Ouija Board Nightmares

The Complete Collection

John Harker

A True Tales 2-in-1 Volume Featuring the Complete Editions of:

Ouija Board Nightmares: Terrifying True Tales
&
Ouija Board Nightmares 2: More True Tales of Terror

ISBN-13: 9781793824585

Some names, locations, and similar identifying details have been changed to protect the identities of the individuals who were either witnesses to or victims of these phenomena.

Table of Contents

Ouija Board Nightmares

Terrifying True Tales

Chapter 1

Mysterious Origins

"Without doubt the most interesting, remarkable, and mysterious production of the 19th century."

– Early description of the Ouija board

In 1890, a group of businessmen led by Charles Kennard of Baltimore, Maryland, decided to act on the rising popularity of "talking boards" among spiritualists. Spiritualism in the United States and Europe had reached a peak in the latter half of the 19th century, with millions of adherents eagerly seeking to communicate with the spirits of the deceased. Frustrated with the slowness of having spirits tap out messages on table tops and/or other antiquated methods of delivery, a group of spiritualists came up with the idea of an alphabet board with a planchette-like device to facilitate message writing from the Other Side. Kennard and his colleagues recognized a niche when they saw one—in this case a need for mass-produced and uniformly-styled talking boards—and thus was born the Kennard Novelty Company.

Making the board was not a problem. But what to call it? The investors decided to ask the board itself. Leading the session was Helen Peters, the sister-in-law of one of the investors, and a known medium in her own right. It didn't take long before Peters revealed what the board had answered: OUIJA. When the group asked what that word meant, the reply came back: GOOD LUCK.

So now the company had a product and a name, but it still needed a patent before it could be offered to the masses. And in order to get a patent, the company had to prove that the board actually worked. That task fell to company attorney Elijah Bond, who took the invaluable Helen Peters with him to the Washington, D.C., patent office. There, the chief patent officer informed them that he would grant the patent if the Ouija board could accurately spell out his name, which was supposedly unknown to Bond and Peters. The board did. Keeping his end of the bargain, the very visibly shaken patent officer granted them their patent on February 10, 1891.

The Ouija board was an instant success. Demand for it was so high that the Kennard Novelty Company went from one factory to seven in a year's time. By 1893, ownership of the company started to change face, and William Fuld, a stockholder and employee, took to running the show. Fuld continued at the helm during the company's boom years, watching as rival board makers launched and failed, none achieving the astonishing success of the Ouija. Fuld died in 1927 after falling off the roof of his newest factory — a factory the Ouija board supposedly told him to build.

In the decades that followed, the Ouija board not only continued its brisk sales, but became entrenched in modern American pop culture. The boards, a mainstay in many homes, could be bought at any neighborhood toy or department store. They appeared in such innocent venues as *The Saturday Evening Post* and the *I Love Lucy* show. They were kept in people's game closets alongside Monopoly and Parcheesi.

In 1966, the multi-million dollar Fuld business was sold to Parker Brothers, which continued to manufacture Ouija boards for the masses in, of all places, Salem, Massachusetts, the site of the famous seventeenth century witch trials. While the 1960s' occult boom added a bit more of an edge to the board, it wasn't until 1973's *The Exorcist* hit movie screens that the Ouija board was cast in a truly sinister light. In the movie, 12-year-old Regan is shown playing with a Ouija board and making contact with a spirit who calls itself "Captain Howdy," Captain Howdy actually being the demon who goes on to possess the unsuspecting young girl. Suddenly the Ouija board wasn't just a harmless parlor game, but rather a portal to hell. Far from slowing sales of the boards, *The Exorcist* actually caused sales to rise, as throngs of curious customers wanted to see for themselves what paranormal experiences awaited them via the "oracle" of the talking board.

Many users, of course, experienced nothing out of the ordinary. If the board did spell out a word or two, it was chalked up to the theory of "ideomotor action," the idea that suggestion or expectation can create involuntary and unconscious motor behavior. In other words, the operators themselves caused the planchette to move around the board, sometimes without even knowing they were doing it. Even today, the ideomotor response is the prevailing theory among Ouija skeptics as to what makes the board "work."

In many instances, this may very well be the case. It's all in the user's head (and out through their fingers, apparently). But it would be a mistake to chalk all Ouija board phenomena up to a supposed dissociative mental state and/or unconscious muscle movement. There are simply too many oral and written accounts by true believers, former skeptics, and paranormal professionals that fly in the face of everything logical and scientific. The stories are endless and range from interesting to horrifying.

The accounts that follow fall on the horrifying end of the spectrum. They are intended to inform, perhaps entertain, but also to warn. You are only asked to read them with an open mind.

Chapter 2

Early Accounts

"Communicating with the dead was common; it wasn't seen as bizarre or weird. It's hard to imagine that now, we look at that and think, 'Why are you opening the gates of hell?'"

– Robert Murch, Ouija historian

The first commercial Ouija boards were an instant hit. For about a $1.50 an average citizen could buy their very own "Ouija, the Wonderful Talking Board" and interact with the spirit world in the comfort of their home. Described by savvy marketers as a magical device that "answered questions about the past, present and future with marvelous accuracy," and promising a "link to the material and immaterial, the known and the unknown," the boards sold like hotcakes and were commonly used by people of all ages, occupations, classes and creeds.

Literary Musings

Author Sax Rohmer had a specific question for his Ouija board in the early 1900s. How could he best make a living as a writer? The board spelled out CHINAMAN. Rohmer soon went on to pen *The Mystery of Dr. Fu Manchu* in 1912 under the pseudonym Henry Ward. That novel and the many others that followed in the series made Rohmer one of the most successful and well-paid authors of the 1920s and 1930s.

In the case of author Pearl Curran, the Ouija board not only gave her ideas for books, but actually wrote the books for her. Curran made headlines in 1916 when she claimed that her stories and poems were dictated through a Ouija board by the spirit of a 17th century Englishwoman named Patience Worth. A spirit with apparently a lot to say, Patience/Pearl produced seven books in addition to volumes of poetry, short stories, plays and other writings between 1913 and 1937, many of which were critically lauded.

Murder, Mayhem and Madness

While the Ouija board was helping some creative types reach artistic success, in other corners of the country it was playing a role in much darker stories.

In New York City in 1920, the police found themselves inundated with "tips" from well-meaning amateur sleuths who were using their Ouija boards to solve the mysterious murder of card player Joseph B. Elwell. (The case remains unsolved.)

In 1921, a Chicago woman tried to explain to authorities that spirits from a Ouija board had told her to leave her mother's dead body in her living room for 15 days before burying her in the backyard.

In 1930 in Buffalo, New York, two Native American women were tried for the murder of Clothilde Marchand, wife of the famous sculptor Henri Marchand. Using a hammer, the elder Indian woman fatally beat Clothilde, believing her to be a witch who had killed her husband. She was told this, she said, from the spirit of her husband whom she contacted through a Ouija board.

In Arizona in 1933, 15-year-old Mattie Turley shot her father to death after being told to do so by a Ouija board. Mattie and her mother had been using the board to help her mother choose between Mattie's father and a handsome young cowboy she had recently met. The board replied with the command to kill Mattie's father with a shotgun. When Mattie was later arrested, she reportedly stated: "The board could not be denied."

In 1935, Mrs. Nellie Hurd of Kansas City received messages via her Ouija board that her 77-year-old husband, Herbert, was having an affair with a neighbor and that he had hidden $15,000 somewhere on their property. When a private detective couldn't prove any of these claims, Mrs. Hurd once again consulted the Ouija board, which then told her to torture a confession out of Herbert. After several nights of being pistol-whipped, tied to his bed, burnt and stabbed, Herbert managed to grab a pistol himself and killed Nellie in self-defense.

Mass Hysteria

Early in its existence, the Ouija board was suspected of causing mental disturbances in many of its users. In 1924, the Swedish-American psychiatrist Dr. Carl Wickland wrote that he had treated the cases of "several persons whose seemingly harmless experiences with automatic writing and the Ouija board resulted in such wild insanity that commitment to asylums was necessitated."

In 1944, Manly P. Hall, a noted occult authority and the founder of the Philosophical Research Society, stated in *Horizon* magazine that "during the last 20-25 years I have had considerable personal experience with persons who have complicated their lives through dabbling with the Ouija board. Out of every hundred such cases, at least 95 are worse off for the experience."

One of the most spectacular episodes in the history of "Ouija board madness" occurred in March of 1920, when police in the town of El Cerrito, California, were forced to arrest seven people who supposedly were driven insane after playing with a Ouija board. A national news headline read, "Whole Town 'Ouija Mad.'" One fifteen-year-old girl, who was found naked and acting crazy, explained that her strange antics and nakedness allowed her to "communicate better with the spirits."

In the immediate days that followed, the madness spread like wildfire through the town and even affected a police officer, who stripped off his clothes and ran into a bank while screaming hysterically. Town officials acted quickly and brought in a bevy of mental health professionals to examine the town's 1,200 residents. Several people were sent to asylums. The professional diagnosis was one of "shared hysteria," but officials took no chances and banned Ouija boards within the city limits.

Chapter 3

Unknown Visitors

"You could be thinking you are speaking to your deceased loved one when in reality you might be speaking to something that has never walked the earth in human form."

– Ed Warren, famed demonologist

There is a scene in the movie *The Exorcist* where Chris (Ellen Burstyn) asks her daughter Regan (Linda Blair) if she knows how to use the old Ouija board she finds in the basement. Regan says yes and that she'll show her.

Chris: Wait a minute, you need two.

Regan: No ya don't. I do it all the time.

Chris: Oh yeah? Well let's both play.

[the planchette is jerked away from Chris]

Chris: You really don't want me to play, huh?

Regan: No, I do. Captain Howdy said no.

Chris: Captain who?

Regan: Captain Howdy.

Chris: Who's Captain Howdy?

Regan: You know, I make the questions and he does the answers.

Questions and answers. They are the essence of a Ouija board session. While it is always clear who's doing the asking, it's often far from clear who—or *what*—is doing the answering.

The Phone Call

In 2005, in a town just east of Salt Lake City, a group of teenage girls decided to try out a Ouija board for the first time "just to experience the phenomenon." They gathered in the living room of Vicki's house (because it was deemed the creepiest) and prepared by lighting candles, designating one girl as a "scribe," and turning off their cell phones so as to not "disrupt the atmosphere."

They started the session and soon started talking to a girl named Wisty. They also contacted a man who would not give his name but who kept pushing the planchette wildly around the board. Tiring of these antics, the girls decided to stop when suddenly Angie's cell phone rang. Not only was it startling because the phone had supposedly been turned off, but also because it used the factory set ringtone instead of the song clip ringtone it was normally set to. Angie answered with a tentative "Hello?" On the other end a man started speaking in a language Angie had never heard before. She told him she was going to hang up. He paused for a few moments and then started laughing. Angie quickly hung up, and that was the last time the girls ever used a Ouija board.

The Sleepover

Beth was hosting a sleepover for some of her close friends. One of the friends arrived late, having just come from her uncle's funeral, and she brought her Ouija board with her. The friends gathered around the board and, at exactly 12:00 a.m., made contact with a spirit. When asked who it was, the board spelled out the initials of the deceased uncle. Thinking that one of her friends was joking around, Beth put the board to a test. She told the spirit that they would all leave the room for three minutes. When they returned, she wanted proof that the spirit was there. The girls left, and after three minutes, Beth rushed back into the room before the others and saw all the proof she needed. All the cupboards were open; dishes were turned upside down; a box of mints had been poured out on the floor in the shape of a star; and the room itself was freezing. The girls attempted some more communication with the spirit after that, but at exactly 2:00 a.m. it moved the planchette to GOODBYE.

The Incubus

Adam, his brother, and their visiting older cousin, Jim, were looking for something to do one summer night in Pocatello, Idaho. Jim claimed to know all about Ouija boards and offered to make one out of cardboard. The next night the boys and a few friends gathered together in the basement, lit some candles, and started playing with the artistically-crafted homemade board. A lot of fooling around ensued, but then suddenly the temperature in the room dropped dramatically and the pointer started to move. Jim asked, "Are you here?" The pointer moved to YES. Then he asked for a name. The pointer spelled out INCUBUS. "Are you an angel or a demon?" Jim questioned further. DEMON, came the reply.

At that point, one of the boys announced in a scared voice that he was through. But the pointer immediately moved to the word NO. Just then a cold wind swept through the windowless basement and blew out all the candles. The terrified boys screamed while Jim made his way to the light switch. When the lights came on, the boys were horrified to see the pointer standing up by itself! Jim grabbed the board, took it outside, and tossed it in a burn barrel.

The next morning Adam's mom opened the front door on her way to the garden and nearly tripped over something lying outside the door. It was the Ouija board. This time the boys threw the board back in the barrel, splashed it with lighter fluid, and set it on fire. While it burned, the boys held hands and recited the Lord's Prayer. To this day, they swear they heard screams coming from the barrel as the board slowly burned.

The Dog Knew

On a cold March night in 2005, Molly and her friend decided to play with Molly's Ouija board. Facing each other in a candle-lit room, the board between them, and Molly's dog to the side chewing on a toy bone, the girls asked if there were any ghosts present. The pointer immediately slid to YES. Then Molly's friend asked the board to prove it. Within seconds, the dog jumped up and started growling at the front door, fur raised and teeth bared. The girls opened the door and looked outside, but saw nothing out of the ordinary. When they came back in, the candles were out and the dog was back to chewing contentedly on his bone. Unfortunately, later that year Molly's dog died of cancer.

A Scary Encounter

Katie was 18 in the summer of 1997. She lived with her mom and sister in a creepy old house in Ohio. As Katie explained, "I lived there my whole life, and all of us experienced seeing shadow people, hearing voices, and things moving on their own. I always had this unnerving feeling that something malevolent was there."

One night some friends came over to Katie's with a Ouija board. They tried to get her to play, but she wanted no part of it, and instead sat at the far end of the room by herself. The rest of the group began asking the board questions, and before long the planchette started to move. It spelled out the name EDWARD. They asked if he was a bad spirit and the planchette moved to YES. Katie at this point thought the others were moving the planchette themselves, but they insisted they were not. Then the planchette spelled out Katie's name. When the group asked "Edward" what he wanted with Katie, he spelled out PUNISH HER. They asked why, and he replied SHE KNOWS. By now Katie was understandably upset and begged her friends to stop the game.

But instead, a boy in the group asked the spirit to prove it was really there. Chaos ensued. The temperature in the room dropped to freezing. The lights dimmed until they were flickering. A stack of papers on a table next to Katie suddenly flipped into the air and scattered all over the floor. And then came the sound of coins being thrown against the walls.

The group was now in a panic. Katie's sister and another girl grabbed a Bible and started reciting verses. Katie ran to the room where her mom was sleeping, woke her and frantically told her what was happening. Katie's mom grabbed a bottle of holy water and started sprinkling it around the house. The weird activity ceased immediately.

After a scolding from Mom, neither Katie nor her friends ever touched a Ouija board again.

The Arabic Speaker

Faran had always thought the Ouija board was a bunch of nonsense. Then one night he attended a casual get-together and found himself participating in a Ouija board session. Though the group was supposedly communicating with many different spirits, Faran wasn't taking any of it seriously. But then he thought of a way to "test" the board. Faran was a Kuwaiti American living in Oklahoma at the time. Only one other person in the room knew him, and even that person didn't know very much about him. So, in Arabic, which Faran was positive no one else present knew, Faran asked the "spirits" how the brother of a friend passed away recently. The board spelled out CAR CRASH. Faran was slightly shocked, but still not convinced it was anything other than a lucky guess. So then he asked, again in Arabic, how old the brother was when he died. The board pointed to the 1 and the 3. Indeed, the boy had been killed at age 13. After that, Faran was no longer a doubter, but he made sure he stayed as far away from Ouija boards as possible.

Movie Night

On a Friday night in 1997, in a suburb of Cleveland, Ohio, Lilly and two friends were having a sleepover. As often happens at sleepovers, the girls decided to play with a Ouija board. The girls asked the board to give some sign that it had real powers. In reply, the planchette spelled out TV 8 PCP. The girls immediately ran to the TV and turned on channel 8, which was playing the movie *Desperate Lives* and just happened to be showing the scene where actress Helen Hunt takes PCP and jumps out a second-story window. The girls put the Ouija board away after that, but Lilly wonders to this day what might have happened to them had they continued to use it that night.

The Doll

C.J., his brother, his dad, and his best friend were trying out a Ouija board in the basement. Before they started, they moved a creepy-looking porcelain doll out of the area and put it in an adjoining room face down on some towels. They then started the session but soon grew disenchanted as they continued to receive nonsensical answers to their questions. C.J. got up to use the bathroom while the others continued playing. As he left he heard them ask the board who was in the other room. When he came back he found the others ready to give up because the board wasn't "working." They showed him the answer to their last question, which was just a list of numbers. C.J. couldn't believe his eyes: the numbers were his social security number!

The men then started asking more questions, and after receiving an answer that C.J. would die in the Air Force, they asked the board to prove itself. That's when it spelled out DOLL. Immediately they went to the other room to check on the porcelain doll they had placed there earlier. When they opened the door, they found to their horror the doll standing upright and staring right at them! Terrified, they ran from the house.

Later on, C.J.'s friend burned the board but went on to have some psychological problems for several months. C.J. actually did join the Air Force. His condition remains unknown.

Message for a Skeptic

On Halloween in 2012, a paranormal group was investigating the local city hall for evidence of supernatural activities, present or past. Kate and a colleague were assigned to cover the story for their radio station. They took a seat in the back and watched as a professional medium directed a group of volunteers in the use of a Ouija board. After a short while, Kate's colleague shuddered and whispered, "Kate."

"What?" replied Kate.

"I don't know. I'm just hearing Kate . . . Kate."

A minute later, the medium, while never touching the Ouija board herself, asked out loud, "What is your name?"

The upturned glass the volunteers were using spelled K8, K8.

The two reporters were understandably shaken for the rest of the evening. And after that, Kate never quite looked at Ouija boards in the same skeptical light.

Jack is Back

When Doreen was 14, she attended a sleepover birthday party during which the girls played with a Ouija board. For about an hour after the session started nothing much happened, so Doreen wandered off to another room. Soon after she left, her friends yelled out that a new spirit named Jack was with them and that it was looking for her. Doreen returned, curious, as she didn't know anyone, past or present, with that name. But Jack seemed to know a lot about Doreen and revealed intimate details about her, including some abuse issues, that she had never shared with anyone at the party. Doreen begged her friends to stop playing, afraid of what else Jack might reveal. Her friends ended the session.

A year later Doreen was at another Ouija board get-together. Only one other girl from the first party was there, and she and Doreen were together in the kitchen when someone yelled out from the other room, "Who's Jack?"

The Floating Ouija

In early 1991, Jane, her boyfriend, and another friend gathered around a Ouija board in a well-lit room, placed their hands lightly on the planchette, and began asking silly questions. They were having a good time, even getting some answers in return, when suddenly the planchette started circling wildly around the board and then slowly lifted up! The trio rose with it, keeping their hands on the topside only, and followed as it led them in a random pattern around the room. Finally the planchette gently landed back on the board and began spelling out words in an undecipherable language (later thought to be Aztec-related). Then, switching back to English, it indicated that it wanted Jane's boyfriend and other friend to leave the room, leaving Jane alone with the board. At this, the three of them jerked their hands away. As if in response, the planchette suddenly went flying off the board and crashed into a wall so hard it cracked the wall paneling and its own plastic exterior.

The next day, Jane called someone familiar with the occult to come and take the board away to "purify" it. As far as Jane knows, it's still in storage somewhere, sealed up safely, and as far away from Jane as possible.

The Little Girl Who Lived Down the Lane

One evening in the year 2000, J.P. and a group of three or four friends were gathered in a basement to "mess around" with a Ouija board. They quickly contacted a spirit who told them her name was Emily and that she was six years old. Emily also told them that she was good. They asked a few more questions, keeping them simple as if they were talking to a real six-year-old, and then someone asked how she died. The spirit spelled out MOM. At this point J.P. got the eerie feeling that he knew who this spirit was. So he took his hands off the board and proceeded to ask questions he knew the answers to. Did the girl have siblings? YES. What color was her house? BLUE. What street did she live on? LOOMIS. The answers lined up perfectly with a murder that had occurred in town the year before. J.P. was well familiar with the story, as he had lived a mile down the road on the same street.

More than a little creeped out at this point, the group politely asked Emily to leave. She replied that she didn't want to. The group insisted she go, wished her the best, and ended the session. As they came up out of the basement, they noticed that the door to an old playroom that hadn't been used in years was wide open. Peering inside, they saw several toys outside their box, lying there like they had just been used.

The Face in the Wall

Todd and Tony were best friends in high school, and one of their favorite things to do together was "talk" to spirits using a Ouija board. That is, until they had an experience that made them never want to be near one again.

It was the middle of the afternoon, and Todd had invited his friends Tony and Sam over for lunch. After a while, Todd took out the Ouija board and he and Sam sat down to play. Tony watched from the couch. Five minutes into the session Tony started screaming, "A face! A face!" Todd and Sam looked over and hardly recognized their "tough guy" friend, who was screaming and crying, an expression of pure terror on his tear-stained face.

After he calmed down a bit, Tony told Todd and Sam he saw a face coming out of the wall behind them. Just then, the phone rang. It was Todd's mother's cousin, who was a priest. Father Dan called rarely, and when he did, it was usually in the evening when he knew Todd's mother would be home. Todd immediately told the priest what had just happened and asked him if Ouija boards were "for real." Father Dan told him that, yes, the boards were evil and that he should get rid of it immediately. Their conversation ended shortly and Father Dan never did ask for Todd's mother. To Todd, it seemed that Father Dan called at that exact moment because he had been inspired to for some reason.

Todd, Tony and Sam are in their 20s now, and a lot of their high school memories are a bit faded. But there is one memory that for Tony will remain as clear as the day it happened—the face that came out of the wall.

Chapter 4

Dark Predictions

"The only one who can reveal hidden knowledge besides God is the devil."

– Fr. James LeBar, exorcist

Zozo and the Grieving Sister

Holly and her two sisters had always been interested in stories of the afterlife and otherworldly phenomena. When they were in high school, the girls bought a Ouija board and started using it on a regular basis. The girls were ecstatic when their first attempts at contacting spirits were successful. According to Holly, they communicated with several spirits who told them all about their past lives, their families, and so on. But after a few weeks, the friendly spirits disappeared and were replaced by something much more sinister. It called itself Zozo, and said it was a devil. It also told the girls repeatedly that it was going to "get them."

Understandably upset and also curious, one of the girls asked their parish priest about the name "Zozo." The priest reacted with an angry outburst, demanding that the girls immediately stop playing with the Ouija board. It was not a toy, he warned, and would only get them into serious trouble. That Sunday, the priest devoted his sermon to the topic of Ouija boards and the occult. Taking the warning to heart, the girls stopped using their board.

A year or so later, a friend of Holly's lost her sister in a van accident. The friend, Anna, knew about Holly's Ouija board experiences and begged her to try to contact her sister through it. Holly hesitated at first, the memory of the scary encounter with Zozo still fresh in her mind. But finally, wanting to help her grieving friend, she agreed. The two girls pulled out the board and almost immediately made contact with a spirit that identified itself as Anna's sister. Anna was overcome with emotion and declared that she didn't want to live without her sister. She loved her so much, she sobbed, that she only wanted to be with her, wherever that was.

Two weeks later, Anna was killed in an accident. A van accident. Holly threw away her Ouija board and hasn't touched one since.

Who Will Die First?

Former police officer Darrell Smith will always remember his one and only Ouija board encounter. It happened in the winter of 1987, in a small town in Iowa. One night he was at his friend Mark's apartment when three neighbor girls came over, bringing with them a Ouija board. The girls started acting out scenes from a horror movie that featured the Ouija, but unknown to them, Darrell had also seen the movie and called them on it.

The girls laughed it off and then urged Darrell and Mark to try it themselves. With a "what the heck" gesture to each other, the two men sidled up to the board and placed their hands on the planchette. They were determined to show the girls that the board did not work. The first few questions they asked of the board elicited no responses. Then they asked, "Who in this building is going to die first?" To their surprise, the planchette moved and spelled the name LARRY. Darrell was speechless. Larry was Darrell's best friend, and he knew without a doubt that neither he nor Mark moved the pointer on their own.

The next summer, Larry was killed in a one-car accident.

The Boyfriend

Karen's great aunt Mary had never married. Curious as to why, Karen asked a relative for some details. The story she was told was shocking. When Mary was sixteen, she asked a Ouija board if she and her boyfriend, whom she was pretty serious with at the time, would get married. The board answered NO. She then asked if they would break up. Again the board answered NO. Then Mary asked if one of them was going to die. The board answered YES. When she asked which of them was supposed to die, the board answered GOODBYE.

A week later Mary's boyfriend was killed in a woodchipper accident at the mill where he worked.

Grandpa

It didn't take long for Matt and his brother to receive a

response from the Ouija board they were playing with one night in mid-2007. A spirit that called itself Seth answered the brothers' challenge to prove it was real in a dramatic and scary fashion. It told them that the grandfather of Matt's best friend would die within a week. Then suddenly the chandelier above the table began to shake violently. The room became as cold as an icebox, though the thermometer read 70 degrees. And a horrible stench like that of rotting flesh filled the room, causing the brothers to cough and gag.

As suddenly as it started, the chandelier stopped shaking. The boys raced to open a window in hopes of dissipating the rotten smell. They ended the night with a mutual pledge to forget what had happened and to never use the Ouija board again.

Their attempt to forget would have been better aided had not Matt's friend's grandfather died later that week.

The Terrifying Messenger

When Carl was a teenager he invited some friends over to play with his Ouija board. They soon made contact with an entity that called itself a demon. The boys asked it a bunch of questions, but the spirit only addressed Carl. It told him it would visit him later after midnight. Scared out of their wits, the boys ended their session and put the board away.

At a few minutes past midnight, just as it had promised, the "demon" awoke Carl out of a deep sleep. It sat on the end of his bed, grinning at him. Carl later related that the creature was small, ugly, and evil-looking. The thing told Carl that his first child would die, and then mysteriously vanished.

The next morning Carl threw the board out in the trash. But a couple of days later a little black boy whom Carl had never seen before came to the house carrying the Ouija board. He handed it to Carl, saying, "This is yours," turned around and left. Now totally terrified, Carl tried to burn the board, but no matter how hard he tried he couldn't get it to catch on fire. Finally, he dug a deep hole, put the board in with a bible on top of it, and covered it back up. That seemed to do the trick, as Carl has not seen the board since.

Unfortunately, the demon's prediction did come true. Carl's wife miscarried their first child at three months.

The Car Crash

When they were about 14 years old, best friends Tami, Jane and Sara got together every Friday night for a Ouija board séance. One night the board was particularly active and told the girls that Jane's brother would be in a car crash. The girls were so scared they called the local hospitals for news of an accident. When Jane's mom heard all the commotion, she came down from her bedroom and warned the girls against having any more séances or she would ban them from seeing each other. They tried to warn Jane's brother, but he just laughed them off.

Three weeks later, Jane's brother was in a friend's car when the car hit a telephone pole, throwing him eight feet into the air. While sustaining severe injuries, his fate could have even been worse had he not changed seats right before the crash.

A Disturbing Dream Come True

When Claire was a teenager in the early 2000s, she had a series of dreams in which she saw herself and her best friend, Ginny, using a Ouija board and communicating with a spirit named Ethan. The dreams were so vivid and intriguing that they prompted Claire to buy a Ouija board and try it out for real. She invited Ginny and another friend over to try it out, not telling either of them about her reoccurring dream.

To guard against unintentionally moving the planchette to letters embedded in her subconscious, Claire acted as secretary, intending to write down what the other two girls received via the board. It wasn't long before the girls made contact with something. Is there a spirit present? they asked. YES came the reply. What is your name? ETHAN, it spelled out.

Stunned and frightened by what she was seeing, Claire frantically demanded that the girls end the session. They moved the planchette to GOODBYE and put the board away. Claire then told her friends about her dream, and the three of them quickly decided to go to a priest the next day for advice.

The next afternoon the girls met with their local priest, who blessed them on the spot in his office and then came out and blessed Claire's house as well. After the blessing, Claire stashed the Ouija board away in a locked cupboard in her basement, with the intention of never seeing or even thinking about it again.

About 18 months later, Claire and Ginny were chatting online on Facebook when suddenly an image of a Ouija board appeared out of nowhere on Claire's laptop screen. She screamed and threw the laptop across the room, effectively smashing it to bits. When Claire's parents rushed to her room, she poured out to them everything that had happened — the dreams, the "encounter" with the Ethan-spirit, and the latest laptop fright. Luckily for Claire, her parents believed her and arranged for counseling for her and Ginny. The family also made arrangements to have the Ouija board in the basement "taken care of" professionally.

Not long after, Claire and her family moved to a new house. They remain hopeful that nothing uninvited moved with them.

A Tragedy Foretold

Paranormal investigator and radio host Paul Eno recounted his own Ouija board experience on his website, *New England Ghosts*. When Paul was a boy in the mid-1960s, he and a friend tried out a Ouija board that his friend received as a birthday gift. The boys were amazed that the planchette was indeed moving around in response to their questions, and after a while they asked a big one: When were they going to die? The board told them Paul's friend would die in 1985 and that Paul would live longer. On that dour note, the boys put the board away and never played with it again.

Unfortunately, Paul's friend did indeed die young, in a scuba diving accident. In 1985.

A Fiery Prediction

Geri only used a Ouija board once, and in this case, once was enough. During the session, attended by a few close friends, the board told Geri that she would die in a fire. Later that night, Geri's mom awoke from a nightmare in which she dreamed their house was on fire and that Geri was the only one who didn't make it out alive.

For the next several years nothing worrisome happened. Geri and her mom moved into a new house, and Geri forgot all about the prediction. Then one night while Geri was sleeping, flames from a forgotten candle left burning on top of an entertainment center escaped their glass container and set the cabinet on fire. Geri woke up briefly when she heard a dog barking, but thinking it was a neighbor's (it actually was her dog), she fell back into a deep sleep. Moments later, Geri's mom arrived home and was able to douse the fire before any major damage was done. Geri and her mom immediately remembered the prediction from years ago and strengthened their resolve then and there to never touch a Ouija board again.

Death of a Princess

Vince had been, in his words, "messing around" with the Ouija board for a couple of years when he had this frightening experience in 1997.

He was using the board by himself when he challenged it to predict something big or important, like a news event. The planchette in response started moving around until it spelled out DI DIE DI DIE DI DIE DI DIE. Vince, of course, thought the board was telling him he was going to die. Then it spelled out PRINCESS DI DIE. Vince was intrigued but doubtful. After all, Princess Diana was still young and healthy. The board elaborated: CAR ACCIDENT. Vince asked where? PARIS, came the reply. Still skeptical, Vince asked when it was going to happen. The board spelled out OHIO. Vince was a little taken aback. He had a trip planned for Ohio in a few weeks.

Vince took his trip and nothing happened. Princess Diana remained alive and well, and Vince remained skeptical of the Ouija board's supposed powers. He soon forgot all about it.

A month or so later, Vince took another trip to Ohio. One day while watching television with friends, he was stunned to hear the breaking news report that Princess Diana had been tragically killed in a car accident in Paris.

Nebraska Nightmare

Eve, Carrie and Debbie were best friends growing up in Nebraska. When they were about 14 they started experimenting with a Ouija board. At first nothing much happened. They asked innocuous questions and received simple one-word answers back in reply. One night they contacted a spirit that called itself Yuri. They didn't talk to Yuri for long, though, because Eve's father came in and angrily ordered them to stop. He was a religious man and told them in no uncertain terms that he would never have a Ouija board in his house. He then threw it in the outside trash can.

Two weeks later Eve's father came storming in the house and demanded to know why the Ouija board wasn't still in the trash. Not knowing what he was talking about, Eve went out to the garage and was amazed to see the Ouija board sitting on a table! She immediately took it over to Carrie's house, where it stayed untouched for several months. Then one night the girls took the Ouija board to a party where everyone paired up and took turns asking the board questions. When it was Eve's and Debbie's turn, Debbie asked the board when and how they were going to die. The board answered YOUNG. Then it spelled out WATER. The girls were of course upset at this response, but tried their best to laugh it off and eventually over time forgot about it.

Six years later, Eve received the news from another friend that Debbie and her new husband had been tragically killed in a car accident. They had hit a patch of black ice and swerved into the path of an oncoming truck. Eve instantly remembered the Ouija board's prediction. Debbie had indeed been young (20) when she died, and the cause of her death was water, frozen on the road. Eve tries to live each day without fear, but she can't completely stop wondering if she will soon be next.

Chapter 5

Unwanted Guests

*"Using spirit communication devices such as a
Ouija board involves giving permission for an
unknown spiritual entity to partly possess your body
(by inviting them to use your arm and hand). Once
they are in that far, why would you assume they will
leave peacefully?"*

– **Adam Blai, religious demonology and exorcism
expert**

Jail Hysteria

In the summer of 2000, a group of inmates at the Santa Clara
County Jail played around with a homemade Ouija board and
experienced a terror unlike anything their years as street thugs
had ever thrown at them.

The group, comprised of Hispanic gang members all in their
20s, decided to fashion their own Ouija out of the back of a
Scrabble board. They penciled in the moon, sun and alphabet,
and made a teardrop-shaped planchette out of a piece of
cardboard. The next night four or five inmates gathered around
the board in a bathroom, with only the faintest light coming in
from under a door. They prayed to Satan and eventually called
up the spirit of a "woman" who told them she had been

murdered. When they asked how, the spirit spelled out the word "investigate."

On a subsequent night, gathered again in a dark corner of the bathroom, the inmates toyed with the board and soon felt an eerie presence among them. They asked if anyone was there, at which point the cardboard indicator started spinning wildly around the board by itself. The terrified prisoners bolted from the room. After a few moments, they went back in, but one of the men started acting strangely. "I felt cold and bigger," he later reported. "I was filled with anger and talked in this deeper voice I never had." At the time, the other inmates thought he was acting, but by the third day they were convinced otherwise. Three of the men now thought they were possessed by an evil entity. They tore up the board and threw it away.

Soon after, on the morning of August 5th, correctional guards heard screams coming from the cells. Rushing over, they found inmates crying and flailing around, screaming that they were possessed. The actions of the inmates were unlike any the jail personnel had witnessed before.

"The sophisticated inmates generally don't show fear," said a jail spokesman. "Fear is a weakness."

Yet these men were so alarmingly afraid of something that jail officials called in a Catholic priest. When the priest arrived, he blessed all 29 inmates and sprinkled holy water on them and their cells. These actions seemed to calm most of the inmates, but the clergyman still spent the next two days counseling the three men who had been the most overwhelmed by fear of possession. Eventually, feeling less distressed and fearful, the men were able to sleep through the night. They vowed never to play with Ouija boards again.

The Incan Warrior

When Monica was a teenager in the early 1990s, she and her friend Kristi decided to try out a Ouija board that Monica had received for Christmas. They placed the board between them on their knees and had Monica's younger sister act as the secretary who would record the events. Within minutes the planchette started guiding their fingertips around the board, spelling out various words. The board told them they had contacted a spirit called Sevatu, an ancient Incan warrior, and that he wanted to talk to them.

Excited over their new spirit friend, the girls met every day to communicate with Sevatu, delighting in the jokes and questions he put to them. But after a few weeks, the tone of Sevatu's messages changed. They became rude and downright menacing at times. One night he even told the girls he wanted them to "come away" with him, after which the planchette flew out from under their hands and hit a wall.

Not so much excited now as scared, Monica and Kristi decided to take a break from the Ouija. But that proved to not be so easy. Both girls started having nightmares. They got so bad that Monica began sleeping with a crucifix around her neck and a bible next to her in bed. An ominous feeling of being watched troubled them day and night, and they were beset by bouts of unexplained depression.

At around this time, Kristi's boyfriend asked if he could try out their Ouija board. Only too happy to get rid of it, the girls agreed and the next day Kristi started driving to her boyfriend's house with the Ouija board on the passenger seat. After a few miles, Kristi's car began to smoke and sputter. It finally stalled out completely, leaving Kristi alone on a dirt road surrounded by cornfields. Fearful that the Ouija was the cause of her troubles again, Kristi grabbed it out of the car and threw it as far as she could into the corn. When she got back in the car she was relieved to hear it start up without a hitch and without any smoke.

Monica continued to feel "haunted" for about a year after ditching the Ouija board, but eventually the fear subsided. The memory of what happened, though, remained strong enough to keep her from ever touching a Ouija board again.

The Devil's Face

When David was about 9 years old, he and his sisters spent an evening "messing around" with a Ouija board. They asked the board silly questions, but not receiving any answers or experiencing anything creepy, they soon grew tired of it and went to bed.

Later that night, David woke up freezing. He looked at his clock and saw that it was midnight. He turned over on his back and looked up at the ceiling, hoping he would soon fall back asleep. But instead of staring at a blank surface above his head, he saw something terrifying staring down at him. To David, it looked like the devil himself. The color of dried blood, the creature appeared legless but sported a muscular torso. Its face looked like a skull with skin stretched so tightly around it that it could rip apart at any moment. Its eyes were mere burning lights, and protruding out of its forehead were two horns. The thing smiled ghoulishly at David, its already-tight skin stretching even more horribly over its skull-like features. Too petrified to move, David closed his eyes, wishing and praying the hideous image away, until he finally fell back into a deep sleep.

The next morning, David woke up to a perfectly normal bedroom. His digital clock, however, had somehow stopped at exactly 12:00 a.m. It wasn't flashing, like it would be if there had been a power outage. It had simply frozen. His watch had also stopped at 12:00.

Though David related this story ten years after it happened, to him it remains as real as the night it occurred. He has not used a Ouija board since.

The Little Witch

Marie, like David in the previous account, was also young when she experienced a frightening encounter with a Ouija board. Living in Los Angeles, 11-year-old Marie was happy to try to befriend the new girl at school, Anna, whom the other kids considered weird. At the suggestion of her mother, Marie brought the girl over to her house one day after school. Looking through the game closet for something to play, Anna seemed delighted to find a Ouija board. Marie told her she thought that was the dumbest game ever because nothing ever happened. Anna just laughed and said that's because Marie hadn't been using it correctly. She then went on to tell Marie that she and her mother were witches and that she knew how to use the board to conjure up spirits.

Skeptical but willing to go along with Anna's instructions, Marie sat down in a chair in the middle of her bedroom with the board on her lap. She let Anna place her hands on top of her own over the planchette and watched as Anna moved the pointer around in a fast circular motion while uttering strange, unintelligible words. Anna then suddenly released Marie's hands, at which point the planchette flew to the letters M-A-R-I-E. Marie screamed and threw the board to the ground.

More angry than scared, Marie demanded that Anna try that "trick" again, but this time with neither of them touching the board. Anna agreed and told Marie to place the board on the floor with the planchette squarely in the middle. Right after Marie did this, the planchette started moving and once again spelled out M-A-R-I-E. This time Marie was truly scared. She ran to her mother and told her what had happened and how she was afraid of Anna. Her mother took Anna home, but remained doubtful of Marie's story.

Later, after she had calmed down, Marie ventured back into the bedroom where the Ouija board remained where it had been before, on the floor in the middle of the room. Seeing it now as nothing more than a piece of cardboard with a plastic pointer on it, Marie was emboldened enough to try it again all by herself. She sat down, put the board on her lap, and started moving the planchette around in a circle like Anna had done. The response was quick…and terrifying. "I felt an entity so strong and so forceful that it literally threw the board across the room and knocked me out of the chair," she later stated. She ran sobbing to her parents. While still not fully believing her, Marie's mother nonetheless promised her she'd get rid of the board.

That night and for several nights after, Marie slept on the couch. At the end of the week, her parents finally forced her back into her own room. Marie hesitantly agreed, but took her dog to bed with her. Later that night, she woke up to the sound of her dog growling and scratching at the door. The room was freezing, and Marie had the undeniable feeling that she wasn't alone. She also felt something else: an odd indifference. She wasn't really scared; if anything, she was angry. Angry at her parents for making her sleep in that "haunted" room. She slowly got up from bed and walked trance-like to her parents' bedroom. At first annoyed, her parents quickly changed their demeanor when they saw the faraway look in their daughter's face as she pointed at something under their bed.

The next thing Marie remembered was being on the couch with her mother wiping a cold cloth over her face. Her mother told her that she and her dad had become alarmed when Marie didn't respond when they called her name. They believed her now, her mom explained, because when they went into her bedroom, they also noticed how cold it was and how the dog was acting crazy. And as far as what was under the bed? It was the Ouija board! Marie's mom had lied about throwing it away and instead hid it, thinking it was just a harmless board game and that Marie's obsession with it would blow over eventually. The next day, Marie's mother really did throw the board away, and as she did she swore she heard it scream.

Dead Frogs and Nighttime Visitors

In 1975, when Jesse was 14-years-old, her family had just moved into a small apartment complex in Ontario, Canada. One day her girlfriend Darcy came over, and having nothing better to do, the two girls decided to pass the time playing with a Ouija board that Jesse's mother had given her the previous Christmas. They took the board down to the basement and set it on a box between them. Then they placed their hands on the planchette and set about trying to contact the spirit of Darcy's grandfather.

"Grandpa, if you're there, can you please let me know?" Darcy asked. Slowly the pointer started to move around the board. At the same time the temperature in the basement became noticeably colder, even though it was a hot July afternoon. The air became heavy with energy and the girls felt without a doubt that they weren't alone in the basement anymore. But instead of being scared, the girls were delighted that something "otherworldly" seemed to be happening. They asked a few more questions of the board, but after not receiving any definite answers, the girls grew tired of the game and packed it up. They promised each other they would not talk about their spirit contact to anyone.

Around 7:00 p.m. that evening, Jesse started feeling

extraordinarily tired. She lay down on her bed and fell asleep immediately. But instead of a nice, peaceful slumber, she soon felt the room spinning around her. She struggled to wake up completely, fighting the panic that was setting in as she felt like her spirit was being pulled from her body. She finally awoke, still exhausted, but now also depressed and scared. "It was almost as if an evil black cloud was around me," she recalled.

Needing to talk to someone, Jesse walked down the block to the nearest pay phone to call her best friend, Tom. On the way there she saw some frogs on the side of the road. Somehow she just *knew* that when she came back, those frogs would be dead. She reached the pay phone and called Tom. He told her to get rid of the Ouija board immediately. The boards are evil, he said. He further instructed her to paint a red cross on it, break it in half, and then throw it away. Jesse went home (passing by the frogs that were now indeed dead), painted a cross on the Ouija board with red nail polish, broke it, and threw it away in a dumpster.

While the Ouija board itself may have been out of Jesse's life, the negative energy she felt after using it lingered for years. Every night at 7:00 p.m., she would feel totally and inexplicably exhausted. When she did go to sleep, she often awoke to her bed shaking or to the frightening feeling of invisible "beings" surrounding her and placing heavy, yet unseen objects on top of her. She also experienced an inordinate amount of bad luck, and one seemingly bad event after another.

Having had enough finally, Jesse one day took out a small

Bible that she'd had since grade school and started praying, or in her words, *begging*, for help. Suddenly, a change came over her, and she felt a peace she hadn't experienced for years. She never again had a 7:00 p.m. extreme-fatigue episode again, nor did unseen visitors terrify her anymore at night.

Nostalgic Nightmare

Mike and Susan were enjoying a night of reminiscing with a couple of old friends. Drinks flowed freely and laughter was abundant. Someone in the group suggested they play with a Ouija board, as they had done in their younger days. After all, it had always been good for a laugh back in the day. Not having one readily available, they made due with cut out letters and numbers, and used a spare glass turned upside down as a planchette.

For the first half hour nothing happened, much like their past unsuccessful Ouija sessions. They were just about to call it a night when the glass suddenly moved. The women accused the men of moving it, but the men vehemently denied any trickery. The glass started moving again, this time slowly spelling out I AM NOT and DIE. The fear-filled looks on everyone's faces pretty much eliminated the possibility that anyone at the table had caused this. All of a sudden, the air was filled with a loud cracking sound and the smell of something burning. The foursome ended their Ouija session and began putting things away. When Mike lifted the table up to put it back in its place, he nearly dropped it in disbelief: on the previously unmarked underside of the table, there now appeared a large scorched area intersected by claw marks.

The group immediately took the table outside, chopped it up, and threw the pieces along with the homemade Ouija board into a raging fire. Unfortunately, things didn't end in the blaze.

For the next two weeks, Mike and Susan reported a barrage of terrifying paranormal events. Their house developed cold spots, unusual for the normally warm interior. At night, knocking and scraping sounds could be heard within the walls. Objects were moved overnight, like pictures that were upside down when Mike and Susan awoke in the morning. But most terrifying were the manifestations both of them saw. Mike claimed that at least twice he saw black shadow "things" dart through the hallway. Susan said she awoke one night to see two tiny eyes staring at her from across the room.

Since neither Mike nor Susan had any religious affiliation, they decided to contact a white witch for help in getting rid of whatever was in their house. After a cleansing ritual was performed, the couple reported they were no longer bothered by any troubling phenomena. They also vowed to never touch a Ouija board again, no matter how strong their nostalgia took hold.

The Haunted Apartment

In 1991, Cassie moved into a Reno apartment next door to a funeral parlor. One of her favorite activities was having friends over and playing around with a Ouija board. Nobody thought it was for real, Cassie recalls. It "was just a fun game." Soon, though, some not-so-fun things started happening. "We heard noises all the time. Scratching, scraping, moaning throughout the living room and kitchen." Even more disturbing, Cassie's five-year-old daughter would come and stand at the edge of her bed every night at 3:00 a.m. and scream until Cassie woke up. At first, Cassie didn't link these strange events with the Ouija board or to anything supernatural. She simply thought her daughter was having difficulty getting used to a new place, and that the strange sounds were due to an old heating system and rusty pipes. That theory was soon to be put to the test—with horrifying results.

Cassie had to go out of town for a few days and asked some friends to stay over to watch her place and take care of her pets. When she returned, her friends weren't there. She finally reached them and found that they were distraught with fear and angry at her for not telling them her house was haunted. They told Cassie that they went to sleep that first night only to be awakened a short time later by a dark, shadowy figure who was standing at the side of the bed staring at them. They immediately jumped out of bed and ran out of the apartment. They never returned and made clear to Cassie that they never would.

After that incident, the scraping and crawling noises in the walls and ceilings intensified, and would last every night from midnight to 5 a.m. At the urging of her friend, Cassie contacted a local Catholic priest, who came over that same day and blessed the entire apartment with holy water. He told her she needed to get rid of her Ouija board and that in all likelihood she had unwittingly attracted some entity from the neighboring funeral parlor. Later, she and her friends tried to break the board but couldn't. They threw it away in a dumpster a few miles away instead.

Cassie moved out of that apartment soon after. She hasn't had contact with the new tenants and so doesn't know—and doesn't want to know—if anything strange and unsettling still exists there or not. But she does know she will never touch a Ouija board again.

A Lack of Respect

Jennifer prided herself on being "a pure atheist materialist," so when her best friend got out her Ouija board one night during the girls' sophomore year of high school, Jennifer made great pains to demonstrate that she thought the whole thing was a bunch of superstitious nonsense. As they got the board ready, Jennifer joked and taunted the supposed spirits, letting "them" know she thought the entire activity was dumb. Jennifer's friend, who took the Ouija board more seriously, tried to tell Jennifer to follow the "rules," like saying "break" before taking your hands off the planchette. You had to show respect, her friend insisted. But Jennifer just laughed this off too.

When the girls at last settled down and placed their hands on the planchette, Jennifer was startled to feel the planchette move without any effort on her part. But she quickly chalked it up to either her friend initiating the action or their collective subconsciousness causing the movement. As the evening progressed, strange messages continued to come through which Jennifer's friend attributed to spirit contact.

Still skeptical, Jennifer was in the middle of making snide comments about the supposed otherworldly being in their midst when the phone suddenly rang. It was about a half-hour after midnight, and the loud, shrill ring unnerved the girls, as no one should have been calling at that time. Jennifer's friend picked up the phone and started to say "hello," when she abruptly stopped, hearing nothing but a dial tone. Jennifer took the phone from her friend, intending to switch off the ringer. She nearly dropped it in fright when she saw the ringer was already off.

Several weeks passed before the girls decided to try the Ouija out again. Jennifer's friend brought the board over to Jennifer's house, but they never got around to it that night and Jennifer just assumed her friend took it back home with her. Shortly thereafter, Jennifer was awakened one night around 3 a.m. to the sound of violent thrashing to the side of her bed. Sleepily assuming it was her cat playing with one of the stuffed animals Jennifer kept on the floor, she turned on her lamp and reached across the bed to shoo him away. But what she saw was a motionless pile of stuffed animals and pillows . . . and the cat asleep at the foot of her bed. With a shaking hand, Jennifer tossed each item in the pile aside until she got to the bottom.

There lay the Ouija board.

The rest of the year proved to be awful for Jennifer. She was involved in multiple car accidents, suffered bouts of severe depression, felt an impending sense of doom and fear, and, contrary to her normal disposition, found herself lashing out at people and thinking the most hateful things.

It took several more years and a conversion to Christianity before Jennifer actually attributed her streak of "bad luck" and dark moods to the Ouija board. Even after converting, it still took some time to believe that a $20 cardboard game from Target could be dangerous. But the more she studied and talked to other people who'd had similar experiences, the more certain she became that she had been under a spiritual attack, stemming from that night when she showed "no respect."

Chapter 6

Physical Attacks

"The Ouija board is a vehicle which makes it easy for negative spirits and demonic forces to enter this plane of existence."

– Anne Rose, psychic and medium

The Whisperer

On an Internet discussion board, a user writes: "I will never again play with one of those boards." She goes on to tell her story of how after using the board "with results," strange occurrences started happening in her home. Floors would creak when no one was walking on them, doors would close by themselves, and there was an unmistakable feeling of being watched. To further make her question her sanity, the Ouija board itself would disappear for days on end, then show up in the most unexpected places.

Eventually the eerie events progressed to where someone–or something–was whispering the woman's name, shaking her bed, and pulling off her covers. On occasion she saw a black mass in the corner of her room. At other times it would be the shadow of man standing in a doorway. But things came to a head when the entity, whatever it was, began physically assaulting her by pulling her hair, scratching her, and even choking her while whispering Latin in her ear. At that point the woman had her house blessed, after which she reported that no other strange phenomena occurred.

Elder Abuse

Jean's mother, Mae, started using a Ouija board shortly after the death of Jean's father. Her mother said she wanted to contact her dead husband and soon became obsessed with using the board, especially after making contact with "spirits" who alleged to be Mae's husband and members of his family. At first the spirits were friendly and pleasant, but after time their demeanor changed. They became abusive and insulting. They even threatened to kill Mae, who by now had quit using the Ouija only to discover the entities didn't need it to communicate anymore.

Jean lived far away from her mother, but when she visited she could see that Mae was being tormented by "something." Mae told her that the spirits are always around her and show themselves as little flames of light. They have used foul language that Jean said her mother would never have even known! And Mae showed her injuries on her body that she said the spirits inflicted on her.

Jean's mother is in her early seventies. It seems the Ouija board doesn't care if the user is young or old. The forces that drive it are, after all, ancient and ageless in their own right.

The Latin Lesson

Riley and a group of college friends gathered around a Ouija board one winter evening, bored but also a little curious. Riley kept his distance, as he was skeptical and more interested in imbibing liquid spirits than talking to dead ones. Soon, though, contact with "something" was made and the board started spelling out words in Latin. Only one person present knew Latin, and that was Riley. He bent over the table to read the words, resting his hand on the table's edge, nowhere near the planchette. When he pulled his hand away from the table, he was surprised to see a fresh scratch on his wrist. For several days after the contact, Riley's girlfriend, who had also been present at the session, woke up with unexplainable bruising on her legs. They both decided that would be their one and only encounter with a Ouija board.

Father Patrick's Warning

Roman Catholic exorcist Father Patrick (not his real name, since his alter-ego as a parish priest dictates the need for privacy) frequently speaks to high school youth groups about the dangers of the Ouija board and other occult practices. He tells one story about a student who contacted him shortly after going off to college. "I'm so glad I got a hold of you, Father," the student began. "You were right. We were messing with a Ouija board last night and in the morning, I woke up with scratches all over my back."

Father Patrick's talks drive home one central message: Dabbling in anything occult, even just out of curiosity, is very dangerous. "There's nothing good that ever comes from that, there is nothing safe about it," he says. "It's a dimension you have no control over. Evil wants to convince you that you will have control over it, but you won't. It's always a mistake."

The Yard Sale Demon

Abby and her mother, Rose, loved to spend Saturdays during the summer shopping at yard sales. One warm and sunny morning in August of 2008, they came across a sale that wasn't on their planned itinerary, but which looked interesting enough to stop at anyway. While Rose rummaged through a box of used DVDs, Abby wandered over to a table of games and puzzles. One in particular caught her eye: a glow-in-the-dark Ouija board. Abby couldn't resist. She snatched it up and brought it over to her mother. "It's only two dollars, Mom. C'mon, it'll be fun to use tonight at the sleepover." Abby's two best friends, Denise and Emma, were coming over that evening to spend the night. Rose hesitated for a moment – anything having to do with the supernatural gave her the creeps – but eventually relented, and the two returned home with two movies, a pair of designer jeans, and a mint-condition Ouija board.

Home alone in her bedroom, Abby tried out the board but soon gave up when nothing happened. She pushed it under her bed and turned her attention to getting ready for her friends' arrival. The three girls spent the first part of the evening eating pizza and cake pops, swapping gossip about their classmates, and watching one of the DVDs Rose had bought earlier that day. Then they retired to Abby's bedroom and got ready for bed. Emma was the first one to flop on the floor, and she quickly noticed something new under her friend's bed. "When did you get this, Abby?" she asked, dragging out the Ouija board. Abby explained about the yard sale and how when she got home and tried it out nothing had happened. "You probably need more than one person," said Denise. "Let's do it now." Abby and Emma quickly agreed.

Deciding that they wanted to make their Ouija board experience as "real" as possible, the girls lit candles, darkened the room, and sat in a circle on the floor around the board. Then they got down to business by putting their fingers on the planchette and asking the board if any spirits were in the room. The answer was immediate. The planchette spelled out YES. Next the girls asked, "Who are you?" HELL, came the reply. At this, the girls recoiled and drew back their hands. Abby wanted to stop playing, but Denise insisted they would be okay if they just commanded the spirit – or whatever it was – to leave. "Leave now!" Denise said in a loud voice. There was no answer. The girls repeated the command. This time the planchette moved to the word NO. Emma, with tears running down her face, moved away and huddled in a corner. Abby wanted to do the same, but she wanted to get rid of the spirit first. She decided to try a religious angle. In a shaky voice, she said, "In the name of Christ, leave!"

Suddenly a shriek emerged from Emma. Still huddled in the corner, she was now cradling her left arm, on which were clearly visible scratch marks that hadn't been there before. Abby started to move toward her, but was stopped when something hit her in the face. She looked down at the object that had assaulted her and saw a little green plastic soldier, one of many that belonged to her younger brother. He had been playing in her room earlier in the day and apparently left some of his toys behind. But who threw it? She looked over at Denise, who clearly hadn't thrown it, as her fingers were still frozen to the planchette.

Just then, the bedroom door flew open and Abby's mother, Rose, came rushing into the room. Perhaps it was the swish of the door–or perhaps something else–but the candles suddenly all went out. Rose quickly turned on the light and asked what was going on. She had heard Emma's shriek all the way downstairs. The girls told her what had happened and begged to sleep downstairs in the living room. Rose agreed without hesitation. After getting the girls settled and attending to Emma's scratches, Rose took care of cleaning up the bedroom and throwing the Ouija board in the trash. Luckily, no other disturbing events occurred in their house after that night, but Rose and Abby vowed to stay clear of any yard sale items that had anything at all to do with the occult. No matter how good the deal seemed, it wasn't good enough.

The Strangler

Cynthia reluctantly agreed to accompany her friend, Tanya, on a double blind date. After dinner at the apartment of their dates, the guys suggested playing with a Ouija board they owned. Tanya was up for it, but Cynthia hesitated. It was the nine-month anniversary of the death of her father and she was feeling depressed as well as a little apprehensive about "reaching out" to a spirit world on this particular night. The others went ahead while Cynthia sat back and watched.

They darkened the room and Cynthia immediately felt as if the oxygen had been sucked out of it. One of the men asked the board who it wanted to speak with, and the planchette spelled out Cynthia's childhood nickname. At this, Cynthia jumped up and said she wanted to leave right there and then. No one except Cynthia herself knew about that nickname. But the players continued, next asking the board who was there with them. It spelled out the name of Cynthia's father. Cynthia was now beyond upset and yelled out "liar!" at which point all the candles in the room blew out. Tanya screamed out next, because she suddenly couldn't move her hands off the planchette. Neither could the two men. At the same time, Cynthia felt an invisible entity choking her. She fell to the floor, writhing in agony and calling out for her father to help her.

While pandemonium was breaking out inside the apartment, a male friend of Cynthia's, Rick, who had prearranged to pick up the girls at 8:00 p.m., came by and heard the screaming from inside. As soon as he opened the door and ran in, there was a tangible "rush" of something leaving, after which everything returned to normal. Rick picked Cynthia up from the floor and carried her out to his car. Then he went back in and got Tanya.

The men from the apartment tried to contact Cynthia and Tanya afterward to apologize and talk about what had happened. The girls, though, wanted nothing more to do with them or the memory of that night.

Nasty Nick

Father Richard (not his real name), a priest on staff at the Pontifical North American College in Rome, recalled an incident a few years ago that involved a 16-year-old girl who came to him for help. She admitted she had been playing with a Ouija board and had seemingly contacted an evil spirit that called itself Nick. Nick would tell her to do things that were blatantly dangerous, such as driving her car in a rainstorm without the windshield wipers on. While she could ignore these suggestions, she couldn't ignore the outright attack that happened to her a few weeks later. She woke one night to find herself surrounded by an impenetrable, "heavy" darkness that was physically choking the air out of her lungs. Just as she was about to give up, the sensation lifted and the darkness cleared. Terrified, she contacted Father Richard the next day. The priest said a prayer of deliverance over her and instructed her to get rid of her Ouija board. Happily, the negative entity never showed itself to the girl again after that.

The God Question

After dinner and drinks in an old hotel on the south coast of England in 1997, two female work colleagues found themselves in conversation with two hotel staff members. The topic at that late hour was the hotel's haunted reputation. One of the women suggested putting it to the test by holding a séance with a Ouija board. As they didn't have a formal board, the group improvised with Scrabble letters and an upturned glass. They started the session with the usual question, "Is anyone there?" There was no immediate reply, and as time passed it seemed there wouldn't be. But then suddenly one of the women, Claire, felt a strange sensation, like a haze had descended upon her. And then the glass began to move.

"Who are you?" a member of the group asked. The glass moved over letters that spelled out the last name of one of the staff members present. Understandably upset, he removed his fingers from the glass, but then the glass moved again over the same letters.

Claire still can't explain what moved her to ask the next question: "Is there a God?" In response, the glass started moving in figure eights, slowly at first and then working itself up to a frenzied pace until it was knocking letters off the table. The terrified group abruptly ended the session. Claire and her friend went to their respective rooms, hoping to shake off the evening's disturbing events with a good, deep sleep.

However, as Claire was about to climb into her bed, something struck her hard in the back. Somehow she sensed that it was not a human intruder that had attacked her, and she lay paralyzed with fear, unable to even utter a sound. After what she deemed a safe amount of time, she attempted to raise herself up, only to be struck again, this time much harder.

Knowing innately that the entity in her bedroom was evil, she began to pray to God in her mind. Almost immediately she felt what she described as a "pulling sensation." She collapsed on the bed and could feel without a doubt that the "thing" had gone. Thinking back on the events of that evening, Claire came to the conclusion that she had been inspired to ask the question

"Is there a God?" during the Ouija session in order to receive an answer that, while harsh, provided her with faith that has lasted to this day.

The Red-Eyed Shadow

Jenny's father was addicted to the Ouija board when she was very young. One day her concerned mother hid the board in a closet. By this time, though, Jenny's father was so adept that he could write the alphabet on a piece of paper and just allow his eyes to spell out words he was guided to see. His makeshift "board" soon told him where the real board was hidden.

Later, when Jenny was four, her father conjured a malevolent spirit that stayed in their house and caused eerie disturbances. Jenny's father was finally persuaded to give up his Ouija board practice when either this spirit, or another, came to Jenny one night in a dream. She dreamed of seeing a one-foot tall shadowy figure with red eyes sitting on her lamp staring down at her. She awoke from the dream only to find the same dark figure actually in her room and on her lamp, looking at her with glowing red eyes. Frightened out of her mind, Jenny jumped out of bed and ran into the kitchen. The thing followed and tried to block her path. Crazy with panic, Jenny managed to veer around it and ran to her parents' bedroom. For some reason the entity did not cross the threshold into the bedroom. Jenny believes it's because her father was in there, and that he somehow commanded "respect" from the shadow figure.

Jenny didn't have any more experiences with the red-eyed

phantom after that night, and to this day has trouble remembering any other dreams.

A Party Gone Terribly Wrong

Lon is a paranormal researcher, writer, and empath who shared his own Ouija board horror story with his readers on his website, *Phantoms and Monsters*.

When Lon was in high school back in the mid-1970s, there was a party one night in the basement of a friend's house. It was a good-sized gathering, as kids from several different high schools showed up. Though the group was underage, beer and wine flowed freely. In the middle of the room, a group of about six kids were gathered around a Ouija board. Lon couldn't hear what exactly was going on or being asked, but it soon became apparent that something was happening. One of the girls was visibly upset and started complaining loudly that someone or something was whispering in her ear and had grabbed her breasts. Lon also noticed that a guy sitting across from her was grinning maniacally and looked like he was about to jump across the table and attack her.

Lon became worried for the girl's safety and locked eyes with the grinner while saying to himself, "Stop now!" The grinner seemed to become suddenly enraged and rushed toward the couch Lon was sitting on, nostrils flaring and the grin now turned to a scowl. The girl sitting next to Lon screamed as the attacker reached out his arms. Lon was able to dodge the attack and countered by pulling the guy down to the couch and holding him in place. Immediately a couple of other men raced over and helped Lon. The attacker quickly calmed down and was visibly shocked by his own behavior, apologizing profusely.

That would have been a disturbing enough note to end the night on, but just a few minutes later a scream erupted from the Ouija board table. Lon looked over and saw to his amazement the planchette hovering completely on its own about two feet above the table. Everyone in the room rushed to the most distant point in the basement to get away from the floating object. Then suddenly the planchette crashed down to the table with a frightening amount of force, breaking one its legs and sending glasses and bottles flying in all directions. The party ended quickly after that as the kids raced out of the basement . . . and never returned.

Lon later shared that some of those in attendance continued to be haunted by the memory of what happened that night and experienced difficulties in life they attributed to the malevolent entity that had been summoned through the Ouija. As for Lon, he regularly tells any and all who will listen to avoid the Ouija board, or any "spirit" board at all costs. Because otherwise, he warns, the costs will be high.

Chapter 7

Lessons Learned

*"In the worst cases, stopping board use and even
getting rid of the board does not stop the activity,
for the spirits are able to literally jump ship and
attach to people and the environment."*

**– John Zaffis, Paranormal Investigator and
Demonologist**

A Father's Warning

Helen had always had an interest in the afterlife. It started
when her father died when she was a young girl. "One night I'd
dreamed my dad wouldn't be around to see Christmas," she
said. "A few months later he was diagnosed with cancer. He
passed away soon after."

Twenty years later, Helen, now a mother of two, attended a
spiritualist meeting, her interest in such things still strong.
Sitting in the back of the packed hall, she watched as a woman
took the stage and scanned the crowd. Suddenly the woman
locked eyes with Helen and began singing at the top of her
voice the Jim Reeves classic song "Welcome to My World."
Helen nearly dropped the cup of tea she had been cradling —
that song had been her father's favorite. The psychic then quit

singing and told Helen that her father had a message for her: She was not to use a Ouija board. He knew she had been thinking about it, but he warned, "No good will come from it." Once again Helen was stupefied. She had indeed been entertaining the idea of using a Ouija board recently, but had told no one about her thoughts.

Despite her father's warning from beyond the grave, Helen couldn't get the Ouija board idea out of her head. One night while having drinks at a neighbor's house, the topic of the afterlife came up. The neighbors, Rob and Judy Johnson, were oracle board enthusiasts and convinced Helen that she should finally see for herself what it was all about. Helen agreed and the Johnsons went about setting up a homemade alphabet board, complete with an upturned whiskey glass for a planchette. The three then sat cross-legged around the board while candles flickered in the background.

The session started with the three of them placing their fingertips on the glass. Helen immediately felt the glass pulling in different directions, but wasn't sure who or what was causing it. Rob then asked the first question: "Who do you want to speak to?" The glass moved over the letters HELEN. There was a pause and then the glass started moving again. This time it spelled out DIE BITCH. Helen was shocked and told Rob she didn't think that was very funny. Rob was adamant that neither he nor Judy caused the glass to spell that. Quivering with fear, but also curious for more information, Helen tentatively asked, "Who are you?" The glass started moving quickly and gave the message, "I was murdered just like you." Helen asked again, "Who are you?" This time the glass spelled out SATAN. Helen screamed out, "I'm not afraid! To hell with you!" At once, the whiskey glass flew off the table and smashed into the wall. Judy leapt up and turned on the lights. The three stood there silently for a few moments as they tried to collect their composure, until Rob finally spoke up: "We should never do this again."

As frightened as she had been that night at the Johnsons', Helen still wanted to know more about the message that was directed at her. She implored Rob and Judy to try to make contact with the spirit again. They finally agreed, but never were able to summon it. A month or so later, Helen woke up screaming from a terrible nightmare in which she dreamed she was being attacked by a man with a hammer. She knew then and there she had gone too far with the Ouija board and vowed never to use it again.

While sticking to her decision, Helen nonetheless still felt uneasy whenever going out, which she did less and less. She couldn't get over the feeling of being watched, or stalked even. One afternoon, however, she firmed up her resolve and left her apartment to visit her son, who lived several blocks away. She had just passed the stairwell when a voice growled behind her, "Die bitch." Trembling with fear, Helen turned around to see a man in a black shirt emerge from beneath the stairwell wielding a hammer. She screamed as he brought the hammer down on her head, and then again. Somehow Helen managed to scramble past him back to her apartment. But before she could unlock and open the door, she collapsed in a bloody heap.

Helen's next memory was waking up in a hospital with a doctor looking down on her and explaining that she had a fractured skull. Her screams had gotten the attention of onlookers, who had called an ambulance and most likely saved her life. Helen's attacker was nowhere to be found.

Seven years later, Helen still lives with the fear that her attacker could come back at any time and finish what he had originally set out to do. Understandably, her biggest regret is not heeding her father's warning about the Ouija board. If only she had listened.

Never Say "Prove Yourself"

When Tara was 15, she and a friend decided to play with a Ouija board one night out of boredom and curiosity. They didn't have a manufactured board, so they made one out of cardboard and used a small drinking glass as a planchette. After Tara's mother went to sleep, the girls lit candles in Tara's room and placed them in a large circle. They settled themselves inside the circle with their homemade Ouija board and started asking it questions.

At first not much happened. The girls mostly joked around and received some harmless answers to their questions. But then Tara upped the ante and asked the board to prove itself. Immediately every single one of the ten candle around the girls went out. Scared witless, Tara jumped up and turned on the light switch. The girls put the board away and tried to calm each other the rest of the night by telling jokes until they eventually fell asleep with the lights on.

Unfortunately, the candles going out was just the beginning of Tara's troubles. A few days later, her stereo suddenly turned on by itself at maximum volume early in the morning. The following afternoon, Tara and her mother were sitting at the kitchen table when one of her mother's hanging teacups started swinging on its hook. They watched, mystified, as the next one in line started swinging also, then the next, and the next, until all of the teacups were swinging by themselves at a frantic pace. Just when it looked like the cups were going to fly off their hooks, they suddenly came to a complete stop.

Then there were the spiders. For weeks after the Ouija board incident, spiders seemed to be everywhere in and around Tara's house. One night when getting ready for bed, Tara pulled the covers down on her bed only to discover two spiders crawling on her sheets. Two days later, she felt something in her towel after getting out of the shower. Again, another spider.

Things visible were bad enough. But it was things invisible and unexplainable that Tara will never forget, like the unembodied, muffled talking that occurred every night outside her bedroom door—and sometimes from within her wardrobe. Not until the family moved to a new house did Tara finally feel free of whatever had been "proving" itself to her since that fateful night with the Ouija board.

It's Not Your Friend

Josh and Derek were roommates, who one night after getting very drunk at a party decided to fool around with a Ouija board. It was about 4:00 a.m. when they came in contact with a spirit who called itself James. James told them he had died of cancer. This sobered up Josh a bit, as he had just recently lost a friend named James to cancer. They tried to engage the spirit more, but were unsuccessful.

However, this startling revelation piqued the roommates' interest to the point that they were soon using the board every day. It didn't take long before they attracted a frequent visitor to their sessions — a spirit named Chad. Chad seemed friendly from the start and often joked with the men about their girlfriends, their appearances, and other mundane matters. One night Chad spelled out the word CAREFUL. When pressed by Josh what that meant, the board then spelled out POLICE. About an hour later, the police arrived at the men's apartment. They had a matter to discuss with Josh that was cleared up later that night.

Grateful to Chad for the police warning, and eager to introduce his younger brother, Kevin, to the seemingly helpful spirit, Josh set up another Ouija board session the next night, this time including Kevin at the table. After many unsuccessful attempts at contacting Chad, Kevin grew bored and took his fingers off the planchette. Immediately after doing so, the planchette started to move. Josh asked the board if Kevin was the reason it wasn't working that night. The board spelled out YES. Assuming new roles, Derek took over at the table while Kevin grabbed a notebook and pen to record the session.

The session resumed in normal fashion, with Josh thanking Chad for the tip about the police, and a bit of harmless banter back and forth. But then things started to change. The planchette kept moving between the M and the A on the board. When the men told it to stop, it began counting down from 10. Again the men told it to stop, and this time it spelled out SO SCARED. A bit wary at this point, but still wanting to know more, Josh and Derek asked who was scared. Once more, the planchette did a frenzied dance between the M and the A, and then began counting down from 10 again. When the men ordered it to stop, it spelled out F**K YOU and called Josh a vulgar name. Having had enough, the men asked the spirit to end the session, but it spelled out NO. They asked again, firmer, and were relieved when the planchette glided over to GOODBYE.

Exhausted and shaken, the men agreed to call it a night. Josh wasn't comfortable staying in the apartment, though, and went home with Kevin, where he slept in the guest room. That night Josh had horrible nightmares. He dreamed of screaming faces that all had blood running from their eyes. He also envisioned a woman cutting her wrists and then slitting her own throat. He awoke in a pool of sweat and slept very little the remainder of the night.

When Josh returned to his apartment the next morning, he was surprised that Derek wasn't there, given the early hour. Around noon Derek came back and explained that when he had tried to go to sleep the previous night, he felt as if there was another presence in the room with him. He tried to shake it off, but it only grew stronger, to the point where he would have sworn a crowd of unseen people were hovering around his bed just watching him. He got up after that and went to his parents' house. But sleep didn't come easy there either. While lying in bed, he saw a shadow figure standing in the bathroom watching him.

The roommates decided on the spot they were done with the Ouija board forever. They broke it up into seven pieces and threw it in a dumpster. Then they asked a clergyman who was a friend of Derek's family to come out and bless their apartment. While these actions provide them with some solace, Josh and Derek still wonder if they've done too little too late.

Should Have Stayed Home

Terri S., now a 30-something adult, has been haunted by a nightmarish experience that happened to her when she was nine years old one warm summer night in Ohio. It all started, of course, with a Ouija board.

Terri's sister, Jill, and Jill's friend Christine, were babysitting Terri when they decided to play around with a Ouija board that Jill had hidden out of sight from her mom's eyes. Terri and Jill's mother had warned the older girls weeks earlier not to play with the board, and had even demanded that they get rid of it. She had assumed—wrongly—that they had.

The girls set up the board in a closet and illuminated the area dimly with some candles. Terri remembers a lot of questions being asked and, finally, a name and an address being given via the board. The next thing she knew, her sister was packing things up, putting shoes on Terri, and rushing them out to the car. Terri was already a little scared at this point, as it was late and dark and her sister was acting too impulsively for Terri's comfort. At last the car stopped; the girls had found the address given to them by the Ouija board.

It was a cemetery.

Seemingly unfazed, or at least not showing it, Jill and Christine marched through the cemetery until they found the headstone with the name on it they were looking for. There they once again set up the Ouija board and candles, and began sending more questions out to the spirit world. Terri sat by an adjoining headstone, waiting patiently for the older girls to finish up. It didn't take long before Terri heard Christine utter a loud gasp in response to a message on the board. Just then all the candles around them went out, but enough light from the moon enabled them to see something that they would not—nor could not—ever forget: the face of a nearby angel statue had turned around to look right at them. The face was phantom white, with hollowed out eyes and a gaping, blackish mouth. Terri's fear at seeing the nightmarish face left her unable to move at first, but hearing the other girls' screams tore her out of her reverie and she jumped up and ran as fast as she could back to the car, trailing Jill and Christine by a hair's breadth.

Many years later, Terri's aunt astonished her by telling her that she had seen that same white, horrific face herself when she was a teenager. It had first appeared in her bedroom window, and several times after that in different places. It was only after getting baptized as a young adult that she quit seeing "the face."

While Terri herself has not seen the face since that eerie night in the cemetery, she has been haunted by its memory, so much so that she has scoured the Internet in search of an image of it, or of anyone's similar tale. Better yet would be an explanation. But Terri knows she probably won't have that any time soon. At least not in this lifetime.

Opening the Wrong Door

Sarah, her two younger sisters, and her mother were having a tough time of making ends meet ever since Sarah's father died in 2008. So it was an unexpected treat when Sarah's mom said "yes" to her daughter's insistent pleas for the last Ouija board on the store shelf in the summer of 2010. With unbridled enthusiasm, Sarah raced to the dining room table when they got home and set up the board. She had just placed her fingers on the planchette and was getting ready to ask if any spirits were present when she heard a loud crash in the garage. The noise startled her so much that she pushed the planchette nearly off the board, where she left it as she and her mother went to investigate the noise.

It was immediately apparent what had caused the clamor in the garage. An old Budweiser clock, beloved by Sarah's father, had fallen off its hook. That was odd in itself, as there was no appreciable cause for its sudden fall. But what was even stranger was that the clock was lying on the floor on the opposite side where it had been hanging. It was as if someone had flung it across the garage, yet there were no scratches or other visible marks on it. Sarah's mom hung the clock back up while muttering "weird" under her breath, while Sarah went back inside to finish her Ouija board session. But another surprise awaited Sarah when she returned. The planchette she knew she had left askew in a corner had somehow been placed perfectly back in the center of the board. This unnerved Sarah enough that she packed the Ouija back in its box and shoved it in a closet.

A few days later, Sarah's mother was outside on the front porch, holding Sarah's baby sister and talking with a neighbor. It was a sunny, warm, and wind-free morning. Suddenly, one of the hanging plants at the far end of the porch flew off its hook and landed at Sarah's mother's feet, giving everyone present quite a scare.

Several months later, just past Halloween, Sarah had a sleepover with two of her friends, Lucy and Anita. The girls decided to watch a movie, so Sarah put on a DVD and turned off her bedroom light. As soon as the light went off, Lucy and Anita let out blood-curling screams. Sarah immediately turned the lamp back on and saw her two friends crying and holding each other tight. When she asked what had happened, the girls said that when the light went out, they saw a tall dark figure — like a man with an incredibly long neck — standing in front of the closet. Terrified, they went back to their own homes and refused to enter Sarah's bedroom after that.

Sarah has reported that many other unexplainable things have occurred in her house ever since bringing the Ouija board home. She often hears whispering voices and footsteps when no one is around, has strange and disturbing dreams, and often feels like she is being watched, even when she is alone. Sarah believes her one and only time using the board opened a door to another world. A world she would just as soon keep far away from hers.

From Bad to Worse

In many cases using a Ouija board only exacerbates an already-present paranormal problem. People often mistakenly think the Ouija will help them find the source of whatever unknown phenomena is plaguing them, but more often than not their good intentions get manipulated by not-so-helpful spirits and backfire on them. The case that follows is a prime example.

* * *

College student Dan couldn't believe his luck when he came across the cool "sorcerer's robe" in the antique store. He had been looking for a Halloween costume, and easily envisioned himself wearing that robe to scads of campus parties. The store owner assured Dan that the robe was an authentic ritual robe over 100 years old and offered him a deal on it that was too good to refuse.

Back at his dorm, Dan hung the robe up in his closet for safekeeping until Halloween. That night, at about 2 a.m., loud crashing and clanging noises roused the roommates from sleep. They ran to the kitchen and couldn't believe their eyes. All the cupboard doors were wide open, their contents strewn across the floor. Not a single pot or pan was where it was supposed to be. The young men had no explanation for what had happened, but since it was the middle of the night and classes loomed early, they shrugged it off as best they could and returned to bed.

In the days and nights that followed, more strange incidents occurred. Lights went on and off by themselves, water faucets were found running when no one was around, rooms were trashed, and the sound of glass breaking was a frequent middle-of-the-night sound. Thinking they had a ghost problem, the roommates decided to try to "contact" it to make it go away. Their tool of choice, of course, was a Ouija board.

Using a board they purchased at a second-hand store, the young men waited until dark and then gathered around the kitchen table where the board was placed. The first question they asked was, "Is anyone here?" Slowly the planchette moved to YES. Then they asked for a name, but all that elicited was the pointer wandering around the board before stopping on a series of consonants. "Are you the one bothering us?" one of the men asked. The response was YES. Finally they asked: "Will you go away?" This time the pointer bypassed both YES and NO and settled on GOODBYE, effectively ending the session.

Far from solving their "ghost problem," the Ouija board session seemed to make things worse, starting that night. Heavy banging resonated from the walls, the sounds of cats fighting filled the air, and an overall oppressive feeling settled heavily upon the dorm. Not knowing what else to do, they decided to ignore the strange activity and hope it went away.

Soon it was time for Dan to go to his first Halloween party, a welcome diversion from the chaos at the dorm. He put on his new robe and immediately felt chilled even though the robe was made of heavy, felted wool. At the party he felt strangely disconnected from everything. He knew people were talking to him, yet their voices seemed far away. But most troubling were the visions he kept having that transposed him to a different place. He saw himself in a dark building lit by torches and candles. He was standing in a circle with other men dressed in robes similar to his. The men were chanting and performing some sort of ritual. Shaken and fatigued by these strange feelings, Dan left the party early.

Chalking up the previous night's experience to his imagination, which he assumed had been stoked by the bizarre happenings in the dorm, Dan went to another Halloween party the next evening. Again, as soon as he put on the robe he felt chilled to the bone. He experienced the same visions as well, only this time they were more intense and vivid. He left that party early too. When he got back to the dorm and removed his robe, the uneasy feeling immediately left him. That was when Dan finally made the connection between the robe and everything strange and unexplainable that had been occurring.

Dan confided in his parents, who put him in touch with a priest and with paranormal investigator and demonologist John Zaffis. Zaffis took the robe from Dan and informed him that it was indeed an actual occult ritual robe with both human and spirit energy attached to it. The spirit energy was dark in nature to begin with, and by using the Ouija board, Zaffis explained, the young men unwittingly increased its destructive powers and allowed it to gain an even stronger foothold in their lives, especially Dan's.

But a positive change came quickly. As soon as the robe was taken away and blessings conferred upon Dan and the dorm, there were no further reports of any paranormal trouble for Dan or his roommates. The robe itself – and the Ouija board the young men used that memorable night – now reside in Zaffis's Museum of the Paranormal, safely bound and de-energized.

Chapter 8

Final Warnings

"The spirit does not have to come right away. It can come after dark to get you."

– Tony Spera, New England Center for Psychic Research

If these accounts have scared the crud out of you, this book has done its job. If you're not there yet, please keep reading. The Ouija board is a dangerous "game." If you have one in your house right now, get rid of it. If you know someone who plays with one, warn them about it. And never, ever get fooled into thinking it's just a way to have some innocent fun.

Ed and Lorraine Warren, in the book *The Demonologist*, describe a case of demonic oppression that happened in the 1970s as "the worst case of diabolical attack [they] have ever experienced." It happened to the Beckford family, and it all began when the teenage daughter started playing with a Ouija board out of boredom. She too was looking to have some innocent fun. And at first it was. But while she thought she was communicating with the spirit of a teenage boy who had been killed in an car accident, she actually was speaking with a demon who was plying her with compliments and empathy while waiting for a chance to gain a stronger foothold. It came when one night the girl asked the spirit to manifest. She wanted to see what he looked like, she implored. Not only did the spirit not answer her, it didn't communicate with her ever again through the Ouija board. It didn't have to. It had acquired the invitation it needed to physically enter the Beckford's realm, and it didn't come bearing gifts. What it brought, with the help of some tag-along "buddies," was vandalism, chaos, and abject terror to the Beckford household.

For 60 days the family suffered through non-stop pounding and other noises, furniture moving around and even levitating, rocks raining down on their house, shrubs torn out of their garden, obscenities written on the walls, pictures falling down, car tires slashed, drawers dumped out . . . the list went on and on. After the bedlam reached a crescendo during Holy Week in April 1974, a priest was called in who performed an exorcism on the house. At one point during the exorcism a horrific black mass materialized in front of the family members and priest. It dissipated and disappeared as the ceremony continued. After the exorcism, a palpable peacefulness and calm presented itself in the house–the first such feeling in over two months. Reportedly, the Beckfords had no further problems. But one can't help think, what if the daughter had never used that Ouija board in the first place?

* * *

That same question could be asked of a 13-year-old boy back in 1940s Maryland. Robbie Mannheim of Cottage City was taught by his aunt, a self-described medium, how to use a Ouija board in the summer of 1948. After several weeks of using the board, strange phenomena began occurring in Robbie's house. Scratching noises were heard within the walls, objects moved by themselves, furniture slid across the floor, pictures would shake and fall off the walls. Robbie himself suffered frequent nightmares and would at times feel scratching in his bed.

In January of 1949, Robbie's aunt died unexpectedly and Robbie, of course, continued to use the Ouija board to try to contact her. Meanwhile the strange phenomena continued, intensified even, and Robbie started becoming more and more agitated and angry. At this point his parents contacted their Lutheran minister, who agreed to observe Robbie in his house for a couple of days. When the minister witnessed chairs moving by themselves, objects flying through the air, and Robbie's bed shaking, he urged the parents to contact a Catholic priest.

Robbie was brought to the office of Father Hughes of St. James Catholic Church in nearby Mt. Rainier. It didn't take Fr. Hughes long to discern that Robbie was possessed, as his telephone and other objects on his desk started moving around during his interview with Robbie, and as Robbie himself spewed blasphemous and obscene remarks at him in an unnatural and guttural voice. After obtaining permission from the bishop, Fr. Hughes had Robbie admitted to Georgetown Hospital, where an exorcism was performed on him. During the ritual, performed by Fr. Hughes, Robbie became violent, spat, vomited, and cast more obscenities at the priest. At one point, he broke loose from his restraints on the bed and slashed Fr. Hughes' arm with a metal spring. After the attack, Robbie calmed down and claimed not to remember anything. He was sent home, but the peace was short-lived.

The strange and scary phenomena continued at home, and Robbie was further tormented by "something" scratching words onto his chest. One of the words was "Louis." When Robbie's mother asked if this meant St. Louis, the word "Yes" appeared in bloody fashion. This prompted the family to visit relatives in St. Louis. A cousin who was a student at St. Louis University talked to her priest professors about Robbie and they agreed to see him. As with Fr. Hughes, the St. Louis priests witnessed the same type of unexplainable happenings when interviewing Robbie. A large bookcase turned around on its own, a stool slid across the floor, Robbie's bed shook as he lay on it, and more obscenities and blasphemies were hurled at the priests from Robbie's mouth but in a voice that clearly wasn't his own. The priests immediately requested permission from their superior to perform another exorcism, and after reviewing all witness statements and medical examination records, Cardinal Joseph Ritter granted their request.

Once again as the priests began the ritual, Robbie became disturbingly violent, growling and screeching, spewing obscenities at the priests, and intermittently laughing in a diabolical voice. The bed he was sprawled on shook up and down, and on his chest the words *hell* and *devil* appeared, scratched into his skin. Because of Robbie's violent reaction to the exorcism, he was transferred to the Alexian Brothers Hospital, where, with the family's permission, he was baptized a Catholic and the ritual continued. On April 18, Easter Monday, the exorcism came to a peak. The records state that it was when the demon recognized the presence of St. Michael the Archangel that it was expelled for good out of Robbie, accompanied by a "gunshot" noise that was heard throughout the hospital. Robbie remembered nothing of the diabolical ordeal other than the vision of St. Michael. He has since remained free of any evil presence.

Author William Peter Blatty heard about Robbie's case in a theology class at Georgetown University. In 1969 he secluded himself in a cabin near Lake Tahoe and tapped out a novel on a green IBM Selectric about a 12-year-old girl who became possessed by a demon. He called the novel *The Exorcist*.

* * *

Malachi Martin, Jesuit priest and author of *Hostage to the Devil*, once wrote that by simply dabbling in the occult or playing around with things such as Ouija boards, séances, tarot cards, and the like, people can open themselves up to possession because they have made themselves "aspiring vacuums" to "whatever happens along."

Ed Warren has called the Ouija board "a notorious passkey to terror." Four out of every ten cases the Warrens have investigated in their career involved people who unknowingly (or in some cases, knowingly) raised inhuman spirits by means of a Ouija board. Some supernatural investigators claim the percentage is even higher. One Catholic website says, "90 percent of their very worst cases involving demonic activity have been linked to the use of the Ouija board."

It's not just Catholic priests and laity who recognize the dangers of the Ouija. Paranormal investigator Darren Ansell has expressed a similar concern. "[I] wouldn't touch a Ouija board with a barge pole," he said. "I've had too many scares over the years." Dr. Alberto Gonzalez, a psychiatrist with the Pan American Institute of Health, has stated: "They [demons] are among us in many instances solely because of these sinister toys called Ouija boards." Dale Kaczmarek of the Ghost Research Society also warns: "This is not a parlor game nor is it something for anyone to experiment with as there are many dangers involved. I constantly get calls and emails from people who are absolutely terrified after using the Ouija and ask for my help. Often this comes in the middle of the night, from out-of-state and by way of adolescents."

Even those involved in the business of contacting spirits *on purpose*, such as professional psychics and mediums, are largely against the use of Ouija boards. As many of them explain, using a Ouija board is comparable to opening your front door and yelling, "Come on in, whoever!"

Psychic medium Amanda Linette Meder gives us this thought on Ouija boards and other divination tools: "Tools for attracting spirits attract ALLLLLL spirits – good, bad, neutral, loving, angry – whatever." Well-known psychic and best-selling author Sylvia Browne states emphatically: "I know you've heard me saying this before, but it bears repeating– never use a Ouija board. They bring in considerable negative energy."

Negative energy, evil spirits, menacing ghosts, demons, devils, or even cantankerous Uncle Gill – no matter what it is that's invoked and invited via the Ouija board, it's not of this realm and it's not your friend. These entities are dangerous, deceitful, and potentially destructive to you and those around you. Why would you invite them into your life?

To be totally clear: Ouija boards are not harmless games. They're not something to play around with at sleepovers. They're not something to buy your children for Christmas.

You've read the accounts.

Please heed the warnings.

"I can hear some of you out there saying, 'Hey, I used a Ouija board and nothing happened.' Consider yourself lucky, then. It's like playing Russian roulette. When you put the gun to your head, if you don't hear a loud noise, you made it. Same thing with the board: The more times you pull the trigger, the more likely that on the next shot, your entire world will go black."

– Ralph Sarchie, former NYPD police officer and current paranormal investigator/demonologist

Selected References

Blai, Adam C. *Possession, Exorcism, and Hauntings.* 2014.

Blai, Adam. "Questions & Answers." *Religious Demonology.* Web.

Bray, Allison. "Exorcists Warn against Buying Ouija Boards as Gifts." *Sunday Independent.* Web. 30 Nov. 2014.

Brittle, Gerald. *The Demonologist: The Extraordinary Career of Ed and Lorraine Warren.* Englewood Cliffs, N.J.: Prentice-Hall, 1980.

Eno, Paul. "Predictions of Death." *New England Ghosts.* Web.

Fulwiler, Jennifer. "The Dangers of Spiritual Glamor (Complete With a Creepy Ouija Board Story)." *Conversion Diary.* Web.

Hsia Chang, Maria. "Perfect Possession." *New Oxford Review* 1 May 2009.

Hunt, Stoker. *Ouija, the Most Dangerous Game.* New York: Barnes & Noble Books, 1985.

Martin, Malachi. *Hostage to the Devil: The Possession and Exorcism of Five Living Americans.* New York: Reader's Digest Press, 1976.

Robert Murch - Ouija and Talking Board Expert. Web.

Rodriguez McRobbie, Linda. "The Strange and Mysterious History of the Ouija Board." *Smithsonian.com*. Web. 27 Oct. 2013.

Sarchie, Ralph, and Lisa Collier Cool. *Deliver Us from Evil: A New York City Cop Investigates the Supernatural*. 2014.

"Satanism Still Strong, Controversial Priest Tells Diocese Crowd." *Los Angeles Times* 21 Apr. 1991. Print.

Saunders, William. "The Exorcist: The Story Behind the Movie." *Catholic Herald* 1 Jan. 1998. Print.

Stites, Roxanne. "Ouija Board Spooks Inmates - Priest With Holy Water Needed." *San Jose Mercury News* 31 Aug. 2000.

Strickler, Lon. "A Personal Ouija Event." *Phantoms and Monsters*. Web.

Zaffis, John, and Rosemary Guiley. *Haunted by the Things You Love*. Visionary Living, 2014.

Ouija Board Nightmares 2

More True Tales of Terror

Introduction

*Enter the world of the mysterious and mystifying
with the Ouija board!*

– Hasbro product description

Since the publication of *Ouija Board Nightmares* in 2015, a lot has happened in Ouija World. In 2016, the movie *Ouija: Origin of Evil* made a modest splash at the box office, raking in over $81 million worldwide, far exceeding its production budget of $9 million. As so often happens with the release of a movie, related items of interest also enjoy a market boost, and the *Ouija* movie franchise is no exception. After the release of the first movie in the series, *Ouija*, sales of the spirit boards increased by 300 percent and became a hot Christmas item that year. Toy manufacturer Hasbro was presumably thanking its own oracle for inspiring them to help finance the movies.

In January 2017, the World's Largest Ouija Board was officially inducted into the Guinness Book of World Records. Built on the rooftop of the Grand Midway Hotel in Windber, Pennsylvania, the board measures 1,302.54 square feet and is visible from Google Maps. The Grand Midway Hotel has had a reputation for being haunted since the 1880s. A gigantic portal to the spirit world on its roof will no doubt help with that little problem.

Personal accounts of Ouija board experiences—some benign, some not so much—have also skyrocketed. People are sharing their stories online, with paranormal investigators and authors, and, when things get really hairy, with their clerics. A campus minister from a college in the Midwest relates that it's not all that unusual for him to find nervous-looking undergrads gathered outside his door on Monday mornings, their worldview in need of righting after a weekend Ouija board session turned their previous perspective on its head.

Then there are the eye-catching headlines that have been everywhere lately. "Demand for Exorcisms on the Rise" (*USA Today*), "Vatican to Hold Exorcist Training Course After Rise in Possessions" (*The Guardian*), "Catholic Church Needs More Exorcists Due to Urgent Increase in Demonic Activity, Priest Warns" (*Newsweek*).

The message in these articles and others like them is largely the same: As more people become involved in occult activities like the Ouija board, Tarot cards, fortune-telling, and witchcraft, as well as non-occult but certainly problematic practices such as drugs and pornography, evil arises proportionately. Sometimes the source of the evil can be directly related to the practitioner himself—for example, an underlying mental illness that is exacerbated by dabbling in any of the above. But sometimes, often times, the evil comes from without, taking the form of an independent, intelligent, tangible dark force that has simply responded to an "invitation."

Father Vincent Lampert, an exorcist in the Archdiocese of Indianapolis, has talked about this correlation repeatedly with various media outlets. In a lengthy interview with *The Telegraph* in 2016, Fr. Lampert warned, "Reliance on pagan activities can create a situation in which evil is invited in." In his experience, the number one cause of such trouble is the Ouija board. "A lot of people have contacted me and said something like, 'We were playing with a Ouija board and all of a sudden our friend starting speaking in this crazy language that we didn't understand. And strange things started happening—things moving in the house'."

The "strange things" that can happen as a result of using a Ouija board range from the milder end of the fright spectrum—unexplained noises, flickering lights, moving objects—to the stronger (i.e., terrifying) end—physical assaults, nightmarish manifestations, and even, although rarely, full-blown possessions. While possessions requiring formal exorcisms are indeed rare, it is interesting that those that do occur are more often than not the result of the Ouija board. Father Thomas Euteneurer, an exorcist and author, has said that as much as 90 percent of the possession cases he encounters began with a Ouija board.

Consider the case of Sean Murphy (not his real name), a father of two who moved from Ireland to London as a young man to work on a building site. One night at a pub he joined a group Ouija session for a laugh. But when it was over, Sean remained intrigued by the board and found himself wanting more. So he started using one at home on a regular basis, and life was never quite the same for him after that. "I had all kinds of troubles down the years and I could never understand the terrible blasphemous thoughts that came into my head." He finally reached out for help after more than a decade of demonic oppression. His exorcism, as he described it, culminated in his being held down by four priests while deliverance prayers were said over his "struggling, screaming body."

Thankfully, Sean's story ended happily and he "felt a new man afterwards" he reported. His case, however, illustrates perfectly the hidden dangers of the Ouija. You may use one once, nothing happens, and you think you've escaped any harm. But this isn't necessarily the case. Just because evil didn't manifest immediately doesn't mean it's not around. Evil is patient. Demons are cunning. They love to deceive. And they will wait.

Hogwash, say the skeptics. The Ouija board is a game, no more dangerous than Scrabble or Clue. If anything "happens," it's because the people playing it have made it happen. Or they have over-active imaginations. Or they're liars. Or they're crazy. Or all of the above.

The skeptics love to raise the theory of "ideomotor action" to explain how words are spelled out on the Ouija board. This theory states that suggestion or expectation can create involuntary and unconscious motor behavior. In other words, when players put their fingers on the planchette (the plastic heart-shaped pointer that's placed on top of the board) and ask questions of the "spirits," it's the players' own thoughts that guide the planchette to certain letters and numbers. Sometimes they know what they're doing. Sometimes they don't.

This could well be the case in many instances. The mind is very powerful. But it doesn't adequately explain all instances of board actions. It doesn't explain how sometimes words are spelled out that are later found to be in a language none of the players know. It doesn't explain how sometimes the planchette moves by itself, with no players touching it. Or how, on occasion, it flings itself off the table, again with no human assistance.

Christina Oakley Harrington, Director of Treadwell's, a London bookshop specializing in the esoteric and the occult, has personal experience with the Ouija and doesn't even try to offer an explanation. "You feel it pulling away from the fingers. I'm not dim—I have a Ph.D.—but it's not being pushed. It's mysterious."

Of course, everyone is entitled to their opinion. But as mentioned in the first volume of *Ouija Board Nightmares*, there are simply too many accounts from too many people—true-believers, non-believers, famous people, average people, young and old people—to claim categorically that the Ouija board is nonsense, or worse, harmless.

As Youth Minister and Pastoral Associate Joel Peters wrote: "A disbelief in something does not necessarily mean that something isn't real. The Ouija board has an objective reality that exists apart from a person's perception of it. In other words, it's real even if you don't believe in it."

For the people whose stories are told in the following pages, there is no disbelief. Many started out as skeptics, but are no more. They know the reality of the Ouija board, and they will carry that reality with them in their psyches for the rest of their lives. Their experiences are related here not only because they are fascinating and thrilling, but more importantly because they serve as a warning.

The message couldn't be clearer. But just in case . . .

> *"Do not play with Ouija boards or let them into your home! Stay the HELL away from that stuff. If you play in the Devil's sandbox, he will take notice of you."*
>
> **– Fr. Scott Brossart, SOLT**

Chapter 1

A Brief Background

The Ouija board was born out of the 19th century Spiritualist Movement, whose adherents believed that not only was it possible to communicate with the dead, but that it was desirable and led to spiritual healing and preternatural wisdom. Frustrated, however, with the slowness of having spirits tap out messages on table tops and/or other antiquated methods of delivery, a group of spiritualists came up with the idea of an alphabet board with a moving pointer to make it easier for the spirits to "talk." Early attempts at constructing the boards were rudimentary at best and remained within the closed circles of the spiritualists.

Businessman Charles Kennard of Baltimore, Maryland, saw the opportunity within this niche and jumped on it. With the help of several investors, Kennard started the Kennard Novelty Company to mass-produce a uniformly styled talking board. In February 1891, the investors obtained a patent for their product, which they called "Ouija, the Wonderful Talking Board." The name "Ouija" came about when the investors decided to ask the board what it should be called. It spelled out the word OUIJA. When they asked what that meant, the board told them GOOD LUCK.

Kennard's hope was that the board would appeal not only to

spiritualists, but also to the general population, and accordingly marketed it as a toy and/or game. His instincts were dead-on, and the Ouija board became a huge success, in time rivaling Monopoly and Parcheesi for space in people's game closets. The rights to make the Ouija were ultimately transferred to William Fuld, a Kennard employee who worked his way up from the ground floor to eventually run the company. Fuld died in 1927, but his company held the rights to the Ouija until 1966, when the estate sold the family business to Parker Brothers. In 1991, Parker Brothers was sold to Hasbro, the current manufacturer and holder of all Ouija rights and patents.

Chapter 2

Strange Events

*"Whatever the truth is, my eyes have been opened to
the dangers of Ouija boards."*

– Zak Bagans, paranormal investigator and host of
Ghost Adventures

Demons of Death

When Mason was 14, he and his younger brother Alex decided
to make a homemade Ouija board just to "mess around." They
drew the letters and numbers in magic marker on a medium-
sized poster board and used a small glass tumbler as a
planchette. Then they spent the next half hour trying to contact
a spirit. Having gotten no responses, they were just about to
give up when the board spelled out SAMAEL. Not knowing
that name, the boys asked who that was. The glass then spelled
out LILITH. Again, the boys asked what the names meant, but
this time the glass went to GOODBYE.

Later that night, about 3:00 a.m., the boys were awakened by a
noise from down in the dining room where they had been
playing with the Ouija. As they entered the room, they couldn't
believe their eyes. The glass tumbler was crazily circling
around on their homemade board. Mason yelled, "Get out!"

The tumbler stopped momentarily, then slowly moved to the number 9. The boys watched in fixated horror as the glass continued moving down the number line until it reached 0. Then it flew off the table at lightning speed and smashed against a wall.

Hearing the commotion, the boys' parents rushed in and asked what was going on. Alex replied that their Ouija board was "going mental." The boys cleaned up the mess, tore the board in half, and went back to bed, hoping for no more paranormal excitement that night. When they awoke the next morning, all seemed well in their world—until they discovered their pet fish and guinea pig were both dead.

Mason later researched the names Samael and Lilith, and now feels that he and his brother could have had a far worse fate than dead pets. In various religious traditions and folklore, Samael is identified as an angel and/or demon of death, and Lilith, one of his many mates, is a succubus known for kidnapping and killing children.

The Warehouse Ghost

Everyone in town knew that the building at the end of Garfield Avenue was rumored to be haunted. Now a warehouse for a landscaping company, it was supposedly the site of an unsolved murder years ago, and it was no secret that employees did not like being alone in the warehouse, especially at night. Kylie's mom worked for the landscaping company, so Kylie heard the stories firsthand about pots getting mysteriously knocked over, workers hearing footsteps when nobody was around, and cold spots suddenly cropping up in the normally temperate enclosure.

While talking about the ghost rumors one day with her group of high school friends, one of the girls made the offhand remark that "somebody should bring a Ouija board into that place." Another girl, Jen, blurted out that she had one at home that they could use. Now they just needed a way into the warehouse. Kylie told her mom what they wanted to do, and to her surprise, her mom agreed to let them in—but she had to be there with them, she insisted.

A few nights later, Kylie's mom led the way to the middle of the warehouse, where the girls sat in a circle surrounding Jen's glow-in-the-dark Ouija board. They began the session by asking if there was a spirit present. The planchette started to move around in circles. Then suddenly there was a loud bang that came from the rafters toward the front of the building. A few of the girls let out a shriek while everyone looked around nervously. After a few minutes of silence, the group decided to continue, a little scared but a little excited too. They asked more questions, with each "answer" coming in the form of a similar bang from different locations throughout the warehouse. Finally, the girls asked if the spirit wanted to harm them. The planchette, which up until now had been moving randomly around the board, suddenly stopped. Then the loudest bang of the night came, and this time it was right above the girls' heads.

The girls screamed and jumped up from the floor. Kylie's mom yelled, "This way!" and led the girls toward the front doors. As they rushed down a long aisle with their flashlights on, they narrowly missed being hit by two large pots that fell from a rack above them. Ten feet further a 40-pound bag of bark dropped to the floor. Just as they reached the entryway, they heard a low grinding noise behind them, but no one dared look back to see what it was.

The next day, Kylie's mom reported that the first worker to arrive at the warehouse that day came across several strange sights. One was a Ouija board lying on the floor in the middle of the building. (The girls had not bothered to pick it up in their rush to get out.) Then there were the shattered pots and tipped-over bags that needed cleaning up. But the strangest of all was a sledgehammer that had been dragged across the dirt-covered floor about twenty feet from its normal spot and left standing straight up. The employee was thinking vandals at first, but that didn't explain how there were drag marks for the sledgehammer, but no footprints.

No Peeking

Derek and his girlfriend, Gina, were sitting on Derek's bed in his dorm room, a Ouija board between them that Derek's roommate had found on the side of the road. When they asked if anyone was there with them, they were delighted when the planchette spelled out ELI. "Okay, Eli, are you a good spirit or bad?" asked Derek. The planchette spelled out DEMON, causing Derek and Gina's delight to dim a bit. But curiosity drove them to keep asking questions. "How many are with you?" asked Derek. The spirit replied, 7. "Which poster is your favorite?" Derek asked. BLOODY MESS, replied Eli. Derek looked up and pointed at a KISS poster that featured singer Gene Simmons sticking his tongue out of his blood-drenched mouth. "This one?" Derek asked. YES, came the reply.

After a few more questions, Derek and Gina decided they wanted stronger proof that "Eli" was real. Derek looked at his collection of skulls on a shelf, positioned so that they faced the door to greet visitors, and told Eli to move them to "prove himself." Eli responded, CLOSE EYES. Derek and Gina did as they were told. When they opened them several moments later, they were shocked to see all three skeleton heads turned toward them. No longer delighted, not even a little, Derek and Gina closed the board and threw it away in a dumpster at the far end of campus.

The Smelly Demon

Paul Roberts, General Manager of Haunted and Paranormal Investigations (HPI) in Sacramento, California, found himself cleaning up a Ouija board mess in 2009 when his office received an emergency call from one very distressed Ted Huntley. Ted was convinced there was a demon in his house, and that the demon took up residence after Ted and three buddies tried to contact deceased pop star Michael Jackson via a Ouija board. According to Ted, shortly after starting the session, a candle they had lit went out on its own, a cold draft entered the room though no windows were open, and one of the men fainted and went into convulsions for two minutes. After their friend recovered (thankfully unharmed), the men packed the Ouija board away and hoped to put the eerie episode behind them.

Unfortunately for Ted, whatever came visiting that night wasn't so eager to leave. The next day, Ted began seeing a shadowy mass in his peripheral vision moving from room to room. Open windows slammed closed on their own accord. And most disturbingly, he awoke one morning to find three circular scratch marks on his leg, for which he had no rational explanation. Ted's religious upbringing kicked in and he suspected he had an evil spirit in the house, no doubt brought in by his ill-fated dalliance with the Ouija board. He called HPI, stressing that he didn't need an investigation—he already knew something paranormal was present—but rather an emergency house blessing. Paul Roberts agreed to come out and do what he could.

The first thing Paul noticed when he arrived at Ted's house was the sickening smell of rotting flesh—a prime indicator of a demonic presence. The smell, which surprisingly was not detected by Ted, only lasted a few seconds but was enough to impress upon Paul the seriousness of the situation. He wasted no time in performing the blessing. Immediately afterward, Ted exclaimed that he smelled a strong flowery fragrance. Interestingly, Paul was the one this time who couldn't detect the odor, but he felt hopeful that this meant the blessing had been successful. According to paranormal lore, when a fragrant odor descends on the scene of a blessing or exorcism, it means the demons have left and angels are now protecting the premises.

A week later, Ted called Paul and reported that no other strange activity had occurred in the house since the blessing. As for the source of the trouble? That had been taken care of too. The same day as the blessing Ted had tossed his Ouija board into the Sacramento River.

Lost Time

Sienna and her friend Hailey used a Ouija board quite a bit when they were teenagers. The girls never took it too seriously; it was more a way to pass time and have a few laughs than anything else. That all changed one night in March 1998, when the girls decided to have a "serious" spirit invoking session. They got started around 9:00 p.m. at Sienna's house, not worrying about how late it might get as Hailey had made plans to sleep over. They dimmed the lights in Sienna's room, lit a couple of red candles, and burned an incense stick to enhance the mood. Then, their hands positioned on the planchette, they asked, "Are there any spirits here?" The planchette started moving under their fingers and spelled out the name PREM. The girls weren't sure if that was just gibberish or a real name, so they asked the spirit where it was from. It answered THAILAND. Then it told them it was there to protect them.

That was the last thing either of the girls remembered. Sienna recounted, "The next thing I knew it's 7:00 a.m.! It's like we blinked and it's morning! We lost 10 hours of our lives!" The girls sat across from each other not knowing what to say or think. It was the most incredible, mind-boggling event either of them had ever experienced.

Hailey never used a Ouija board again, but Sienna did a few times. Thankfully, nothing ever happened like the lost time episode, or anything even remotely close. During the process of getting her thoughts together to retell this experience, she called Hailey (who she has been friends with all this time) to ask her if she remembered that night in 1998. There was a pause on the other end of the line, then a timid "yes," followed by a firmer statement that she didn't want to talk about it ever again. This was followed by an excuse that she had to go and a quick hang-up.

Sienna doesn't blame her friend for wanting to forget that night. She just wishes she knew what happened in the ten hours they can't account for.

The Recycled Ouija

When Kevin was eleven years old, his older brother, Jay, brought home a Ouija board he had found at a yard sale. Jay was so excited about his near-mint condition treasure that he wrote his name in fancy lettering on the back of the board. Kevin thought it looked pretty boring for a game, but agreed to join Jay and their sisters in Jay's bedroom for a "séance." The siblings had barely started asking questions of the spirit world when their mother entered the bedroom unexpectedly and wrenched the board away like it was a bomb about to explode. Kevin could barely remember his mother ever being as upset as she was at that moment. She scolded them roundly and forbade them to ever bring another Ouija board into the house. Then she marched the board outside and threw it into a trash can. The next morning, Kevin was playing outside when the trash pickup arrived and emptied their garbage—Ouija board and all—into the back of a foul-smelling truck. Kevin assumed that would be that last he would ever think about a Ouija board. He was wrong.

Many years later when he was an adult, Kevin's mother called and angrily asked him why she just discovered a Ouija board in her attic. Which one of the children brought it back in from the trash and hid it? Kevin tried to reason with her and told her it must have been a different board. Perhaps it had been there before they moved in. It couldn't have been Jay's, Kevin assured her. He himself had seen it go into the garbage truck more than a decade ago. Then why, his mother asked, did it have Jay's name inscribed on the back of it? Kevin was at a loss for words. He wished he could have asked Jay about it, but his brother had died a few months after the board was thrown out.

Count Your Chickens

When Peter was in his early 20s, he lived in an old farmhouse in central Wisconsin with six other young people. One night, three of them decided to play around with a Ouija board. As they weren't located that far from Plainfield, the home of serial killer Ed Gein, they thought maybe they had a good chance of summoning a restless spirit or two. They set up the board on a table in the living room, dimmed the lights, and lit some candles. They were just about to place their hands on the planchette when, to their amazement, it skittered across the board on its own.

Emboldened by this early success (and feeling safe in numbers), the housemates dived into a lively session with a spirit that called itself, fittingly enough, Ed. This elicited chuckles from the group. "Really? You couldn't be more original?" said Jill, who in addition to enjoying the game was also enjoying her third glass of wine. For the next hour, the entity answered every question put to it, though not always to the participants' liking.

"Who will die first among us?" Peter asked.

JILL, it replied.

Jill looked up, her face a mixture of fear and defiance. "Oh hell no!" she declared. Then the planchette started to spell again. MURDER, it wrote. Jill pushed away from the table. "I need some fresh air," she said as she rushed out the back door.

Peter shrugged and joked with the others, trying to lighten the mood. "This thing's just makin' stuff up," Peter said. Then he challenged the spirit. "Tell us something for real. Something that can be proved."

For several moments there was complete stillness. Then slowly but deliberately the planchette moved from letter to letter. It spelled out BURY THE CHICKENS. The roommates looked at each other, confused. "What does that mean?" asked Peter. The planchette moved again and spelled out FIVE. Just then the group heard Jill yell from outside: "Hey, you guys! Come here!" They hurried outside to where Jill was standing. There at her feet, arranged in a circle, were five dead chickens. There was no apparent cause of death; all looked like they were simply sleeping. "I thought they were, until I nudged one," Jill said.

They went back inside and closed the board. No one ever suggested playing with the Ouija again. Years later, one of the people who had been present that night in the farmhouse, Dan, was committed to a prison for the criminally insane. At the time of this writing, Jill was reportedly still alive.

Underground Fright

Edinburgh, Scotland, is said to be one of the most haunted places in the British Isles. Along its streets are a myriad of hotels, pubs, and graveyards with spooky tales to tell and resident ghosts to claim. But what's on top is only part of Edinburgh's story. Hidden beneath the city is a dark, damp maze of streets, tunnels, and vaults — the remnants of a bygone era that was built over in response to natural disasters, swelling populations, and infrastructural advances. Largely unchanged since the 17th century and earlier, this underground city is considered a hotbed of paranormal activity, and as such has attracted the attention of professional and amateur ghost hunters alike.

Milly was neither when she and a group of friends decided to spend the night in one of the underground vaults. She, like her friends, simply wanted an interesting, if not unusual, evening with a few thrills thrown in if they were lucky. As it neared midnight, Milly and her friend Bridget pulled out a Ouija board. They quickly made contact with something, and started the normal line of questioning such as *Who are you? How long have you been here?* and so forth. The replies were slow and not always coherent, so after about a half hour, Milly asked the board if she could leave. The planchette moved to YES. After ten more minutes, Bridget asked if she also could leave. The planchette promptly moved to NO.

Up to this point, the activity on the Ouija had been fairly lackluster, but after giving its No answer, it suddenly erupted into a frenzy of movement. The planchette moved wildly around the board, Bridget's fingers barely able to stay affixed, while repeatedly going to the word NO or spelling out NO whenever Bridget asked if she could leave. By now the rest of the group had gathered to watch what was happening. People were getting visibly upset, not only by the drama at the Ouija board table, but also by sudden onset of cold air that filled the room. It was only when several people started crying that the entity stopped its vexing behavior and moved to the word Goodbye. Milly, Bridget, and the others wasted no time retreating back to the streets of modern Edinburgh, where most things made sense, even after midnight.

Battleground Tempest

On a hellishly hot and humid summer night in 2003, Atlanta resident Rosa Sanchez and her friends Christine, Jack, and Matt decided to do a little ghost hunting in Atlanta's famed Tanyard Creek Park, the site of a bloody Civil War battle in 1864. Rosa was the paranormal enthusiast of the bunch, but it didn't take a lot of convincing to get the others to go along. Matt was an archeology major, so he was always interested in visiting historical sites, and Christine and Jack were never ones to turn down an invitation that included a bottle of Wild Turkey.

The group drove to the south end of the park and proceeded to walk about a half mile in, where they settled under a trestle bridge that crossed the creek. They all agreed they needed to "loosen up" before trying to contact any ghosts, so they spent the first part of the evening telling stories, catching up on gossip, and passing around the liquor. After about thirty minutes, Matt reached into his pack, pulled out a headlamp, and announced he was going off to look for artifacts.

"Don't you want to talk to dead soldiers with us?" Rosa teased as she pulled a Ouija board out of her backpack.

"Tell whoever I said hi," Matt replied as he trotted off toward the woods.

Rosa set up the board on a flat rock and instructed the others to gather around in a circle and place their fingers on the planchette. "Are there any spirits here with us?" Rosa intoned.

Jack laughed. "Sure there are. We've been drinking them all night."

Rosa gave him a dirty look and asked again if any spirits were present. Growing bored and impatient, Jack started moving the planchette around the board on his own. "Maybe we just have to warm it up a bit," he said.

"Jack, knock it off," Rosa hissed. "You're going to ruin everything."

"Not much to ruin," he muttered, giving the planchette one final push before getting up from the make-shift table and stumbling back to his blanket.

Rosa and Christine decided to try again on their own. They were just about to place their hands on the planchette when, suddenly, Christine let out a shriek and jumped back from the board. Rosa saw it too. The planchette was moving by itself.

Lazily at first, it circled around the board before settling on a letter: M. Again it moved, to the letter A. Then T. Then a loop around and another T.

"Oh my God! Matt!" Rosa whispered. Then, louder, she yelled out, "MA—"

Her shout was cut off by an inexplicable gust of wind so strong that it blew the Ouija board off the rock and smashed it against a tree. The squall continued, violently thrashing tree limbs and making it hard for anyone to breathe. After a few minutes, it stopped, as suddenly and strangely as it had started, and the night reverted to its previous hot and humid stillness.

The silence didn't last long before they heard the crash of something large lumbering through the brush. It was coming toward them fast. They tensed, and then quickly relaxed as the familiar figure of Matt appeared, breathless and clearly shaken. "Am I ever glad to see you guys," he said. "My lamp went out and I couldn't see a thing. And then that weird wind came."

The others looked at each other and silently concurred it was time to go. Whatever they had crossed paths with that night was better left alone. As was the discarded Ouija board, which, not surprisingly, no one went back to get.

Chapter 3
Menacing Messages

"When you use a Ouija board, you are essentially picking up the phone and dialing a random number and giving whoever picks up your address and your social security number."

– Adam Blai, religious demonologist and exorcism expert

The Liar

John and his grandmother were extremely close. She lived downstairs from John and his parents in an old but charming duplex in Pittsburgh. Their proximity enabled them to easily do many things together, but what John enjoyed the most was listening to Grandma's stories about her past and people that she knew, some of whom John also knew, and many that he didn't. One person from their shared history whom John had never met was his Uncle Roy, who had died at birth. One day when John was 15, his grandma invited him down to her apartment and asked him to join her in using a Ouija board to try to contact Roy. She thought that maybe John's youthful energy would help "connect" them to her lost son.

John was happy to help, as well as curious about what might

happen. It didn't take long before they made contact with a spirit who identified itself as Roy. John's grandma was overjoyed. She asked, was he happy? YES, he replied. Was he with his father (who had died ten years earlier)? YES. Did he know who John was? YES. This pleasant interlude continued for a while, but then Roy's answers started to get edgy and, at times, mean. When John asked if heaven was beautiful, the spirit answered back, YOU DUMB SHIT. This took John and his grandma aback, and they started to wonder if it was even Roy they were talking to.

Their question was answered when the planchette started moving faster around the board and told them, I HAVE ROY. And then came this terrifying message: I AM COMING FOR JOHN. That's the last thing John remembered before he blacked out and slumped down on the table. When he came to, about a minute later, he saw a petrified look on his grandma's face and shattered glass all over the kitchen. While he was out, all the light bulbs in the kitchen had exploded.

As John and his grandma cleaned up the mess, they agreed never again to touch a Ouija board. Theirs went out in the trash that day along with the shattered bulbs.

This Isn't Fun Anymore

Nora and her twin brother, Miles, were home on winter break from college when they got together with some friends from high school on a bone-chilling Saturday night. After a couple of hours of talking and drinking, the group was more than ready for Nora's suggestion that they try out a Ouija board that she had discovered in her parents' basement the day before.

The friends settled around a table, with Nora and Miles on opposite sides. Miles spun the pointer around several times to "warm it up," then proceeded with the first question: "Is there any spirit with us now?" Silence ensued for several moments until Nora's friend Sam shouted out sarcastically, "Hell-ooo?", right after which the planchette shot up to the word YES at the top of the board. The piece of plastic had jerked so quickly that Miles' fingers fell off it.

Over the course of the next half hour, the board was extremely responsive. The friends took turns sitting at the table and asking questions. Nora estimated that they collected messages — mostly innocuous — from five women and three men in that time period. But after a while, the responses grew darker. Curse words and threats began to flow, prompting Miles to ask, "Are you good or bad spirits?" There was no answer. Then Miles asked, "Did any of you kill yourselves?" The planchette moved to the number three.

"Tell us how," Nora said. "G for gun, H for hanging." The pointer skittered over to H. Just then the group heard a soft banging sound, not unlike the sound a body would make if it was hanging from a rope and its feet were gently bumping against a wall.

"Why did you kill yourself?" Miles asked the spirit. The word WIFE appeared on the board. "Your wife made you kill yourself?" Miles asked. This time the board spelled out DEVIL.

The friends were silent for several moments, not quite sure where to go with the line of questioning. Finally, Nora cleared her throat and asked the spirit if he hated women. The planchette pointed to YES. Then she asked if he wanted to hurt anyone in the room. Again, YES. When Nora asked how, the spirit spelled out FIRE.

Just then one of the candles that was burning in the room tipped over and splashed hot wax on Nora's leg. Startled, she leaped up from the table and moved over to a nearby couch, her wound inexplicably more like a knife cut than a burn. Though most of them were scared at this point, the friends decided to keep playing. Nora's friend Sydney took her place at the board. Suspecting now that they were dealing with dark spirits, possibly demonic, Miles asked again, "Are you good or evil?" The board answered, EVIL.

"That's it! We need to put this damn board away!" yelled Sam.

Miles ignored him and asked if there was anyone in the room that the spirit wanted to hurt. The planchette spun around several times and then spelled out HAT. Sam, the only one in the room wearing a hat, shot up from his seat, screamed an expletive at the board, and retreated to a far corner.

Nora suggested to Miles that maybe they should put the board away, but Miles shook his head and feverishly asked more questions. The next few answers they received made no sense to any of the group members, but then the planchette spelled out the name of Nora and Miles' father. The siblings looked at each other warily as they decided whether to proceed or not.

Their father was, in Nora's words, "messed up," and they wondered how much family drama they should allow to be made known public. Miles decided for them. "Why are you interested in our father?" he asked. The planchette slowly spelled out DEAL WITH THE DEVIL.

"What?" exclaimed Nora. She knew their father had problems, but what was this supposed to mean? Miles then said, "Be more specific." NO WORK, revealed the board. Miles and Nora went silent. Their father, who was technically disabled, was indeed out of work and receiving government assistance.

Startling them out of their reverie, the planchette started spinning wildly around in circles before seeking out the letters that spelled JOIN ME IN HELL MONT—

Miles violently flipped the board over before it had a chance to finish their last name. The friends were now of one mind. They gathered everything together—the board, planchette, paper on which they had written the messages—and burned it all in an empty trash barrel. After a short period of time talking about what had happened, the group disbanded, everyone a bit more sober and a lot more shaken. Needless to say, there were no more Ouija boards at any of their future gatherings.

I Can See You

Mark was spending the night at his best friend Daniel's house when the two of them and Daniel's sister decided to "goof around" with a Ouija board. At first the only communications they received were gibberish or random words that didn't mean anything. Mark admitted later they were really just trying to scare themselves and have fun. But then a message came through that was decidedly different from the previous blather. It said, I CAN SEE YOU THROUGH THE WINDOW. The trio tried laughing it off, but then another similar message appeared. I CAN SEE YOU THROUGH HIS EYES. Daniel's sister wanted to quit at this point, but the boys convinced her to stay, arguing that they were safer together. Mark then asked the spirit where it was. I'M UNDER THE CAR, came the reply.

Mark still doesn't know to this day how the three of them got up the nerve to go outside and check under the car, but with flashlights in hand, they ventured out to the driveway and peered underneath the parked Ford sedan. They were greeted with a hiss from a huge stray black cat. The petrified teens raced back inside, only to be thrown into a deeper panic when the power suddenly went out, engulfing the house in total darkness. Fortunately, the lights came back on a few minutes later, but for Mark and his friends, there would be no rest that night. They stayed up until dawn together in the same room, too afraid to go to their separate beds. Needless to say, they never "goofed around" with a Ouija board again.

The Abortion

Reuben and his wife, Roxanne, weren't big believers in the supernatural, but when a neighbor gave them a box of board games that included a Parker Brothers Ouija board, they thought they'd see for themselves if the scary stories associated with the board were true.

On a Friday night, about 1:00 a.m., after making sure their three kids were sound asleep, the couple set up the board and attempted to contact Reuben's father, who had passed away six months earlier. They began to wonder if they were doing it right, as the planchette wasn't moving an inch. After about ten minutes of wording their request in different ways, the planchette finally started to move. Reuben asked if his father was present. The planchette pointed to NO. "Who are you, then?" Reuben asked. The planchette slowly spelled out the word BABY. "How did you die?" asked Roxanne. The word it spelled out made Roxanne gasp. ABORTION.

Only Reuben knew that his wife had had an abortion when she was nineteen. He looked at Roxanne, her face ashen and her fingers trembling on the planchette, and knew he should stop the game. But as he later explained, it was like an unseen force was compelling him to stay there. "Just a few more questions, okay, Roxy?" She nodded hesitantly. Reuben didn't have to ask any more questions, though. The board was suddenly a flurry of activity as it spelled out the names of their children along with a number of vulgarities.

Then a scream punctured the night. "Mommy! Daddy!" their oldest daughter cried out. Reuben and Roxanne flew out of their chairs and raced upstairs to their daughter's bedroom. In a state of near-hysteria, their daughter told them a man came through her window and went right through her wall into the hallway. Reuben immediately searched the house, baseball bat in hand, but found no sign of an intruder.

By now the ruckus had awakened the other kids. Reuben and

Roxanne ushered them all into their master bedroom and told them to stay put. Mom and Dad would be right back, they promised, but first they had to take care of something downstairs. With the intention of getting rid of the Ouija board, the couple returned to the living room. What they saw nearly made their hearts stop. On the floor were the dismembered parts of an aborted fetus.

Retching as she backed out of the room, Roxanne ran to her phone and called 911. Reuben again searched the house, maniacally intent on finding the sick creep who had invaded their abode. When his search again ended in vain, he and Roxanne slowly walked back into the living room and found . . . nothing. The bloody spectacle of just moments ago was completely gone. As Ruben later recounted, "It couldn't have been a dream or a hallucination, as we both witnessed the exact same thing."

When the police arrived, they searched the house and yard, but of course failed to uncover any evidence of an intruder. The male officer, Reuben recalled, didn't try very hard to hide his skepticism. The female officer seemed more sympathetic, gazing more than once at the Ouija board while the couple recounted the events of the evening. On the way out, she told them that as a lifetime resident of New Orleans, she's seen many strange things and then quietly urged them to get rid of the board.

Reuben and Roxanne destroyed the board that night, and the next day contacted their parish priest for further guidance. Their doubts about the supernatural now erased, the couple vehemently tells any and all listeners: Stay away from the Ouija board!

The Tester

In the fall of 2000, Mike and Josh dragged out an old Ouija board from Mike's basement and decided to "waste some time playing around with it." Nothing happened for the first fifteen minutes or so except for a lot of laughing and goofing around. Finally the teens composed themselves enough to ask in a serious manner if any spirits were present. The planchette moved to YES and then back to the middle of the board. Mike and Josh started arguing about who moved the pointer, each adamantly insisting it wasn't him.

After they calmed down, they promised each other they wouldn't move it knowingly. Then they asked another question: "What's your name?" The marker glided under their fingertips to a word that looked like nonsense: HRGOFALAR. The boys looked the word up online and found nothing like it. So they asked again, this time phrasing their question, "What do humans know you as?" This time the board spelled out ABADDON. When the boys searched for that name, an entry in the Catholic Encyclopedia came up that called Abaddon "an angel-prince of hell."

Now they were getting somewhere, thought the teens. "So you're a demon?" asked Mike. I AM CALLED MANY NAMES, came the reply. The boys asked it more questions, primarily of a religious nature since that was a topic they frequently talked about and disagreed on. (Mike was a Catholic and Josh was an atheist.) Finally, they asked the spirit what its job was. I AM A TESTER. And then it added, EACH PERSON IS ASSIGNED A TESTER.

Mike wanted to quit at this point, but Josh wanted to know one more thing. "What's my future?" he asked. The board answered, NICK. The boys looked at each other. They didn't know a Nick. "Who's Nick?" Josh asked. The board was silent. Josh asked a different question: "What will happen to Nick?" This time the planchette spelled out PARALYZE. Josh was stunned. "You mean, I will paralyze Nick?" YES, the board answered.

The boys had had enough. They closed the board, and while Mike kept an open mind about whom or what they had been communicating with, Josh was certain it was his subconscious mind that had been at work. Or that Mike had broken his promise and was controlling the planchette. As the years passed, Mike and Josh lost touch with one another. It's unknown if "Nick" ever crossed Josh's path. If so, hopefully not in the way the spirit predicted. Then again, maybe it was just a test.

You Never Forget

Nancy was 15 when she and her older sister Doreen made their own Ouija board one night when their parents were out. The girls drew numbers and letters on a piece of cardboard and used an upturned drinking glass for a planchette. Placing their fingers on the glass, they began their game by asking if anyone was present. Nothing happened for about ten minutes, but then, after repeated questioning, the glass began to move and went to the word YES. Then it kept moving, spelling out words that were nothing but gibberish to the girls, but doing it faster and faster, so much so that the girls had to quit trying to write it all down. When it momentarily paused, Nancy asked the spirit its name. Once again, the glass skated wildly around the board before spelling out GO TO HELL. Then it flew out from beneath their fingers and right off the table.

Nancy recounted that story 50 years after it happened, the memory of it as strong today as it was then. She stated that throughout the years, her sister has always sworn that she didn't knowingly move the glass. Nancy also denied being the "mover," adding that it would have been impossible for her to push the glass around at that speed, as she only had one fingertip on it at all times. In a forum discussing the paranormal, Nancy wrote: "Please be careful . . . I might have been a skeptic then but I am a believer now."

A Horrible Prediction

Edmond Gross, in his book *The Ouija Board: A Doorway to the Occult*, discusses a case that illustrates how addictive the Ouija can be once a "correct" answer is given to astonished participants. It also shows, tragically, how continued use of the board can lead to questions that perhaps are best left unanswered.

During her freshman year at Vanderbilt University in the late 1960s, Cecilia and three girlfriends started playing with a Ouija board for lack of anything better to do. The girls were immediately rewarded for their efforts, with answers coming from the "mystifying oracle" that were amazingly accurate and prescient. In one example, the girls asked what was Brazil's gross national product in 1966. Having no clue if the answer they received was right, the girls later looked it up in their campus library. To their astonishment, the number they wrote down from the Ouija board was exactly what they found in a reference book. They were hooked.

Almost every evening for the remainder of the term, the girls gathered around the Ouija for a question and answer session. One night they finally got their spirit contact to give them its name. GEORGE, it spelled out. Then they asked him where he was from. The board spelled out HELL. The girls were used to a lighter mood during their sessions, but they nonetheless decided to keep going. Keeping with the more serious tone, they chose to ask a more serious question. When were they going to die? George gave dates for all of them. Three of the four were far off in the future, but one, Barb's, was within that year. The girls were too frightened by this point to go on, and in fact stopped playing the board altogether.

Several months later, on the exact date "George" had predicted, Barb was killed when her car crashed through a guardrail on a California coastal highway. Police had no plausible explanations for the accident. Barb had not been impaired in any way, she had no history of depression, and road conditions were fine at the time of the crash. Tragically, she was the only one who knew what really happened.

Other than George.

Aunt Marie

Beth adored her Aunt Joni. Not only was her aunt funny and kind, but she was also young and cool. Unlike so many of her friends' aunts who looked like grandmas, Beth's aunt was only eight years older than she was. They listened to the same music, watched a lot of the same television shows, and loved playing all sorts of board games together.

One night when Joni was babysitting, she pulled out a game Beth hadn't seen before. It was a Ouija board, and judging from the eerie picture on the box, it looked like it promised a creepy good time. Joni said they were going to try to contact her great-aunt Marie, who had been dead for well over fifty years. Beth recalled hearing a few things about Aunt Marie, but no one in her family ever wanted to talk about her for any length of time. Until now.

"Some people think she murdered her fiancé," Joni told her while setting up the game. "His body was never recovered, but there was blood all over a dress the police found that belonged to Marie. She told them it was from a really bad nosebleed. Right after that, she left town. Didn't tell anybody where she was going or why she was leaving. No one heard anything else about her until she killed herself five years later in Chicago. Jumped right out of a Ferris wheel when it was at its highest point."

Joni had finished setting up the Ouija board and motioned for Beth to sit across from her at the table. Beth moved numbly to the chair. She had never heard this story about her great-great-aunt, and she wasn't so sure she wanted to know anything more. But Joni was really excited about trying to talk to Marie and solve a long-held family mystery, so Beth did her best to help out. She placed her fingers on the pointer, like Joni instructed, and tried to concentrate while Joni called out to the spirit world. "Is anyone here with us? Aunt Marie, we call on you to join us."

Nothing happened for quite some time, and Beth was starting to get bored with this new game. Then suddenly the plastic pointer moved under her fingers. She assumed Joni had moved it, but her aunt looked as surprised as she did. "Marie, is that you?" Joni asked. The pointer moved slowly to the word YES. Joni glanced over at Beth and gave her a nervous smile. "It's working," she whispered.

"Marie, why did you leave town?" Joni asked. The planchette remained still, so after a few minutes, Joni asked a more direct question. "Marie, did you kill anyone?"

The answer was immediate. YES. Then just as quickly the pointer skidded over to NO. Back and forth it glided between YES and NO, over and over.

"Stop it!" Joni ordered. "Who did you kill?"

The planchette was still for a moment. Then it spelled out YOU.

Beth whimpered. She wanted to quit, but Joni reassured her. "It's okay. It's lying. They always lie." The planchette started moving again, this time spelling out ME. Then it spelled out, over and over, YOU-ME-YOU-ME-YOU-ME-YOU-ME . . .

Joni jerked back and pushed herself away from the table. "That's it. We're done," she announced. She hurriedly packed the board into its box and gave Beth a shaky smile. "Don't worry, Beth. It's just a stupid game," she told her. They watched television the rest of the night until Beth's parents returned home.

That night Beth was awakened by a noise in her bedroom. She looked up and was horrified to see a ghastly looking woman tapping outside her window. The woman was staring at Beth with coal-black eyes sunk deep within her cadaverous face, yet she was smiling in a wistful sort of way that made Beth think for one odd, fleeting moment that maybe the woman had no evil intentions after all. But then the specter started opening the window, and that's when Beth screamed for her parents. In an instant, the vision vanished.

Beth's parents spent the better part of the next morning trying to convince their daughter that what she had seen was just a dream. By lunchtime, Beth was starting to wonder if maybe they were right. When she awoke the following morning, and the next, without any memory of a late-night intruder, Beth wrote off the vision at the window as simply her imagination.

A dreamy figment is likely what it would have remained for Beth had not she been along to help her dad clean out her grandma's basement six months later. As he opened a large trunk, Beth's dad exclaimed, "Well, hello there, Aunt Marie," and pulled out a gilded frame portrait of a smiling young woman in a blue dress. Beth froze. The woman in the painting was the same woman she had seen outside her window.

Beth remembers Joni babysitting a few more times before the two girls grew older and moved apart. But from then on when Joni came over, she brought only candy and cassettes. And the only board game they played was Sorry.

Chapter 4

Creepy Coincidences

G-O-O-D L-U-C-K

– Meaning of "Ouija" . . . according to the Ouija

Known Before Birth

Lily and her sister were ecstatic when their first attempt at using a Ouija board, a homemade one no less, resulted in a lively "conversation" with multiple spirits. After asking if the spirits were good (YES) and how many there were (2), they asked what their names were. The response was AIDEN and HANNAH. Soon after, the session started to fizzle and the girls closed the board. Later that evening, after telling their mom about their Ouija adventure, they were astonished to learn that "Aiden" and "Hannah" were names their parents had originally picked out for them before they were born.

A Morbid Thought

In 2006, Drew was getting ready to apply to several film schools in southern California. His portfolio already contained a couple of short films, but he wanted to do one more, a spooky bit entitled *Ouija*. Having limited resources, he used his parents' house for the set and enlisted three of his friends as actors. He had his friends sit around a Ouija board in his parents' living room, which was appropriately darkened and decorated with flickering candles, and instructed them to act like they were seriously trying to conjure up a spirit. Drew's friend Blake, however, couldn't make it through a take without laughing. Finally, in a fit of frustration, Drew told Blake to think of something morbid to get through the scene. Think of a dog dying, he said. In fact, think about Salty (Blake's dog) dying. It worked. Blake held his giggles at bay and Drew shot the scene. The next afternoon Blake called Drew to tell him that Salty had been hit by a car and died.

Saved From Vietnam

Many of Leo Borland's memories have faded with time, but there is one from his youth he will never forget. It serves as a constant reminder to Leo that his life could have turned out completely different from the one he's long been thankful for. And it also verifies Leo's belief that there are many things in this world that simply can't be explained by rational means.

It was the mid-1960s, and for young men in the United States it was a time of unease and uncertainty, as every day brought the possibility of being drafted for the Vietnam War. Even though he was too young to serve, it was still very much on the mind of Leo one evening when he and some friends got together and decided to play with a Ouija board. After the usual horseplay during which the boys asked questions about girls and accused each other of moving the planchette, Leo asked if he would be drafted and go to Vietnam. To his relief, the pointer moved to

NO. But then he wanted to know why. The pointer moved over a series of seemingly meaningless letters: SYLVESTRI. Neither Leo nor any of his friends knew what to make of the strange word, and it was quickly forgotten.

One day a couple of years later when Leo was 18 and working at a quarry, a new foreman, known only to Leo as Dan, assigned him to operating a dump truck and uploading rock. Leo was used to driving heavy machinery and eagerly went to work. He began to back the truck up to the targeted cliff when suddenly he felt the ground shift. Panic seized him as he realized the cliff was giving way. With no time to escape, Leo braced himself and prayed as the truck toppled backward over the crumbling cliff and fell 50 feet down. He landed hard. A pain unlike any he'd ever experienced shot through his right leg before, mercifully, he blacked out.

Leo awoke in a hospital in a body cast. The accident had shattered his femur, which had to be reconstructed with a metal plate. It took months of healing before his cast could be removed and he could walk again. If any good could be taken from his horrific injury, it was that Leo's draft number was reclassified and he never had to serve in Vietnam.

Thinking back to his Ouija board session several years earlier, Leo could have easily chalked up the board's correct prediction to a coincidence. After all, the board had a 50-50 chance of getting it right whether Leo went to Vietnam or not. But it was a bit more difficult to find a coincidental role for the word SYLVESTRI, the given reason why he didn't go. In fact, it was impossible to call it a coincidence because, as Leo learned after the accident, Sylvestri was the last name of the new foreman on the site that fateful day.

Bad Luck or Bad Spirit?

Lorena, Mikala, and Libby were inseparable as teenagers. They attended the same school, lived in the same neighborhood, and shared many of the same interests. So during a sleepover one warm August night when Lorena suggested playing with a Ouija board, the other two girls readily agreed. It wasn't long before they were "conversing" with someone or something. They asked innocuous questions and received simple, even dull, answers back. That is, until Libby asked how it had died. MURDER, it spelled out. The girls looked at each other anxiously and then asked how it had been murdered. The spirit answered, NOT I. The atmosphere in the room suddenly changed. It felt heavy and disturbing, as if something ominous had come in and filled the space. Already on edge, the girls froze in absolute fear when the planchette started to vibrate under their fingers. It shook from side to side, faster and faster, and then, like a sideways rocket, shot out from under their hands and sailed across the room. The girls immediately put the game away and vowed to have nothing to do with it ever again.

Unfortunately, whatever came through the board that night was not done with them. Mikala's mom died a week later of cancer. The family was in shock, as nobody even knew of her condition before it was too late. Not long after, Libby's mom was hospitalized for a severe drinking problem, and that same week, Lorena's mother underwent an emergency hysterectomy. Looking back, Lorena admits their mothers' bad fortunes could have just been a coincidence. But ever since that night with the Ouija board, she herself has felt "haunted." For nine years following the spirit session, she has been troubled by disembodied voices, unexplained footsteps, and mysterious shadows slinking around her house. She is still waiting for the "coincidences" to end.

A Teacher's Question

Callie is a retired schoolteacher who over the years has seen and heard many things that have delighted, saddened, and amazed her on more than a few occasions. She is blessed with a sharp, retentive mind, but even so some of her memories are faded and fuzzy around the edges. There is one memory, however, from over forty years ago that is as clear today as it was then. She credits its clarity to her teacher training.

It was the first time Callie had ever seen a Ouija board. A friend had brought it out and convinced Callie to try it out with her. Callie was game for the new experience and began by asking the first question that popped into her head: Who was her guardian angel?

The planchette under the women's fingers began to move. It spelled out J-A-M-E-L. Neither Callie nor her friend had ever heard of that name. The small southern town they lived in was extremely homogeneous, without even any Catholics or Jews residing in it. So a name that sounded faintly Arabic was alien indeed.

Seven years later and now a full-time teacher, Callie found herself once again at a Ouija board session, this time nearly 200 miles away from her hometown. She was merely an observer at this one, but watched with interest as the group made contact with an entity of some sort. The leader of the group asked their "guide" what its name was. It spelled out J-A-M-E-L-L-E.

Callie was dumbfounded, to say the least. Thankfully, nothing nefarious ever happened after these brushes with the paranormal. But even after all these years, the teacher in her wants to know, why the different spelling?

How Many Did It Say?

Lori was in her second year of college when she went to a party one night on campus where the center of entertainment was a Ouija board. Her friend Betty was leading the session and doing the questioning.

"Will I marry John?" Betty asked, referring to her boyfriend at the time.

The planchette moved to YES.

"How many children will we have?"

The Ouija indicated 30.

This elicited boisterous laughter from the crowd gathered around. So Betty asked again, "How many children will we have?"

But the board was firm and once again the planchette moved to 3 and 0.

After that the board went silent, prompting the partygoers to move on to new circles and new activities, the humorous Ouija response already fading from many beer-soaked minds.

Many years later, Lori ran into a couple of her college acquaintances and spent time with them catching up on the lives of mutual friends, including Betty, whom she hadn't seen since graduation. She found out that Betty had indeed married John. When she asked if they had any children, the answer she received left her dumbstruck.

"No, she had three miscarriages and so they stopped trying."

All Lori could think of was the Ouija board from the party so long ago.

30.

Three . . . zero.

In the Air Tonight

Marines are known to be tough, but sometimes even they can be rattled by a brush with the eerie unknown. In 1991, Kirk was 21 years old and stationed at the Marine Corps base in Quantico, Virginia. After one particularly hot and stressful day, he and two of his roommates chose to unwind with some music and a Ouija board. One of them had plugged an old Walkman into a set of speakers and put a Phil Collins cassette on to play. Then they sat around the Ouija and reached out for a spirit. It wasn't long before they got one, a soldier named Bobby from the Civil War, or so it claimed.

The men spent about a half hour conversing with Bobby, trading benign information back and forth, while Phil Collins crooned in the background. The song "In the Air Tonight" had just come on when suddenly the planchette started circling wildly around the board and the temperature in the room dropped to icy cold. Then the planchette spelled out DEMON IS COMING, and at the exact moment it landed on G, the song slowed and slowed until it was so distorted it sounded like a demon was already there.

Kirk swore and jumped up from his seat. The other two men backed away also. They were used to being able to see an enemy coming. This type of encounter they had not trained for. Later when they looked at the cassette player, they could tell that the batteries had died. That at least could explain the song slowing. What still couldn't be explained was the timing.

Secrets of the Lake

One rainy Saturday afternoon when Bobby was ten-years-old, his mother took out a Ouija board from the back of a closet and suggested to him and his sister that they have a little fun with it. With nothing better to do, the kids jumped at the chance to play a new game and spend time with their mom. For the first half-hour or so, the threesome had a rollicking good time, spelling out silly words like "poop" and "booger," all while making no effort to hide their obvious moving of the planchette all over the board.

But then their mom said she wanted to get serious and ask the board about a friend of hers who had recently gone missing. She instructed Bobby and his sister to place their fingers on the planchette and not to move it themselves. Then she spent several minutes asking out loud if any spirits were present. The planchette suddenly lurched to the right. "Hey, don't move it!" yelled Bobby's sister. "I didn't!" Bobby yelled back. Bobby recalled that though he was trying to show bravado as the only male at the table, the movement actually scared him. He knew the planchette had moved on it own.

"Quiet," said their mother. "Don't be scared. Just let it happen." She asked again if a spirit was present. This time the planchette slowly moved to YES. "What is your name?" she asked. The planchette spelled out the name JASON.

Bobby looked at his mother and will always remember how her face turned white before his eyes. "Mom? Is that your friend?" Neither Bobby nor his sister knew the name of the friend their mom was inquiring about. She nodded, and then in a trembling voice asked, "Where are you?"

LAKE.

Their mother abruptly pushed away from the table and announced that the game was over. As she packed up the board, she tried to turn the mood around by lightheartedly declaring the game as "lame," and suggesting they go out to dinner to be with "real people."

Two weeks later, Jason's body was found in a nearby lake. Police speculated that he had fallen into the water after being hit by a car or train on one of the many bridges in the area.

Chapter 5

Infernal Intruders

"You could use the Ouija board today and nothing supernatural may happen, but later—no telling when—the demonic may intrude on your life."

– Ed Warren, demonologist

The Winged Wraith

In the spring of 2003, Australian teenager Lisa Walters and two of her friends conducted a séance using a Ouija board as their chosen means of communication. That was Lisa's first experience with a Ouija, and she remembers thinking during the session that it would probably be her last, as nothing out of the ordinary was happening and, frankly, the whole thing was rather boring. The friends spent more time arguing over who was pushing the pointer around than communicating with any spirits. The séance was quickly forgotten as the girls ended the evening with a movie and then went their separate ways. The Ouija board was relegated to the back of the hallway game closet.

At 3:15 a.m. Lisa suddenly awoke to a feeling of pure terror. Though she could see nothing strange in her bedroom, she felt certain that something was there with her, watching her. She pulled the covers up over her head and eventually fell back to sleep. The next night, at exactly the same time, 3:15 a.m., Lisa awoke again with a feeling of dread. Peeking out from under her covers, she scanned her room and once more saw nothing to explain her fear. Oddly, though, when she looked to her left the feeling of terror intensified. Too afraid to do anything more than retreat back under her covers, Lisa remained in that state, awake and petrified, until dawn.

When the sun finally pierced her blinds a few hours later, she felt emboldened enough to get up and investigate. What was over to the left that gave her such a scare? The only furniture against that wall was her writing desk and chair. Looking around, everything seemed normal on her desktop, but when she pulled open the drawer she was shocked to see the planchette from the Ouija board lying there beside her markers and notebooks.

Lisa shivered uncontrollably. She had no doubt the planchette was the reason for her unexplainable night terrors, but how did it get from the hallway closet to her desk? With a deep breath, she picked up the planchette and carried it out to the trash. She didn't want to think too deeply about what had happened. She just wanted it to be over. Unfortunately, that wasn't to be the case.

At 3:15 a.m., Lisa once again woke up, this time because an invisible weight was bearing down on her from above. The force became so great upon her chest that she was afraid she would soon pass out. She tried to shout, but her voice was as paralyzed as the rest of her. Just as panic threatened to completely engulf her, the weight suddenly subsided. Lisa drew several deep breaths, jumped out of bed, and raced out of her bedroom, the fear of being suffocated outweighing any other concern. She went down to the living room, turned on the television and two lamps, and eventually fell back asleep on the couch. The next morning, suspecting the worse, Lisa looked in her desk drawer and found the planchette in exactly the same spot as the day before. Taking no chances this time, Lisa stuffed the planchette and the Ouija board in a trash bag and walked the six blocks from her house to the nearest commercial dumpster to dispose of the hellish game.

With the Ouija board now safely out of the house and on its way to pulverization, Lisa looked forward to a restful night's sleep. But that night she awoke again at 3:15 a.m., only to be scared senseless by black shadows flitting around her room. She ducked her head back under the covers and remained there until morning. A search of her room the next day revealed no hidden planchette, which she was thankful for, but it was also apparent that neither the planchette nor the Ouija board itself at this point was the problem.

That night and the next, Lisa was awakened at 3:15 a.m. On each occasion she saw dark shadow balls circle around her room and disappear out the window. Other people in the household also began seeing the strange shadows, and not just at night. Lisa's mother thought she saw a moving black mass behind some boxes in the laundry room one afternoon. And both of Lisa's siblings refused to go to the end of the hallway where Lisa's room was located, claiming it was "creepy down there."

As the shadows didn't seem to be harmful, Lisa learned to accept them and resigned herself to interrupted sleep. Then one night, at 3:15 a.m., Lisa's dog woke her up with his whimpering. Assuming he had to relieve himself, she got up and let him outside. As soon as she climbed back into bed, she heard him crying and whimpering outside her window. With a sigh, she got up again and let him back in. He made a beeline for her bed, but as soon as Lisa settled in, the dog began carrying on.

"Ugh! This time you're going out and staying out," she told the dog. She led him down the hallway but stopped when the dog suddenly turned around and started growling. *He sees something behind me. An intruder?* Lisa wondered, panic quickly spreading through her. Slowly, she turned around and saw something she would never forget. A monstrous bird-like figure filled the corridor. Its outstretched wings reached from ceiling to floor and were the only clear feature on the otherwise shadowy entity. It started to move, gliding more than flying, though its wings were still outstretched. With a shout, Lisa ran down the hallway, sensing that the creature was close behind. She glanced back and nearly fell as the thing soared over her head and disappeared into the family room. Lisa's parents, hearing her screams, ran out of their rooms to find her crouched on the floor in near-hysteria. A thorough check of the house provided no clues as to what Lisa could have possibly seen.

After that night, things settled down somewhat for Lisa. She was no longer awakened at 3:15 a.m., nor did she see any more mysterious shadows in her room. After thinking about it years later, she believes whatever "it" was that terrorized her for that short period in her life came into her world through that one use of the Ouija board. Even though the board was discarded quickly, it took awhile for the forces attached to it to leave. Lisa is just thankful that they finally did. And always fearful that they'll return.

A Haunting in Germany

Stephen's father was in the military, and for several years when he was a child his family lived in Germany. Most of his memories are of a carefree, happy childhood. But there was one troubling period he and his sister won't ever forget, and it all started with an innocent curiosity over a Ouija board.

Stephen was 12 and his sister, Jane, was 14 during the time the family lived in a small apartment in Stuttgart. One day when two of her friends were over, Jane devised a homemade Ouija board using a piece of cardboard and a drinking glass. Jane and Stephen's mom had been a Ouija board aficionado in her youth and so had no problem with the girls' experiment. In fact, she ushered Stephen into the kitchen with her to give the girls more privacy.

The kitchen door had a glass insert, so Stephen could watch the girls clearly while sitting at the table and eating a sandwich. He had just finished his snack and was about to go out to the backyard when he saw a man walk past the kitchen door. Stephen froze. Not only was the "man" pitch black with no definable features, but he made no sound, neither by his footsteps nor at the door through which he had to have entered

146

the apartment. Telling himself his imagination was playing tricks on him, Stephen hesitantly inched forward and peered down the hall in the direction the figure had gone. He was relieved to see nothing there, but worried at the same time. Where had it gone?

Just then his sister and her friends got up from their table and entered the kitchen. Jane was excited. She told her mother that they had actually communicated with a spirit. When they asked if it was good or bad, it spelled out GOOD. And when they asked where it was from, it answered NEAR. Then things got a little weird, Jane said. They suddenly felt a draft pass over them, though no windows were open, and then the odor of a burned-out match came out of nowhere, though nothing had been lit. They tried to "talk" to the spirit again, but quit when they received no more answers. Stephen wasn't sure why, but he decided to keep his shadow man vision to himself. He wasn't entirely convinced the specter had actually left their home.

It wasn't long before Stephen's worries proved credible. Lights started going on an off by themselves, doors opened and closed, and shadows flitted around doorways and in the corners of rooms. Sometimes the family would hear footsteps in a room that was completely empty and knocking on doors that had no one behind them. Usually these strange occurrences happened at night and were most often witnessed by Stephen and Jane. But one afternoon their mother asked, "What's that smell?" and proceeded to walk toward the bathroom to investigate. Stephen and Jane smelled it too. It was unlike any odor they had ever smelled before. Seconds after reaching the bathroom, their mother rushed out, coughing and gagging. She slammed the door shut and called the superintendent, thinking maybe there was a sewer leak in the pipes. By the time help arrived, the smell had vanished. Stephen remembers his mother muttering, "It was like something died in there."

The most terrifying episode, however, occurred one night when Stephen was lying on his bed reading a comic book. Someone, or something, pushed up on his mattress from beneath the bed. Stephen remembers being so scared that he screamed at the top of his lungs, causing his worried parents to rush into his bedroom. For the next two weeks, Stephen refused to sleep in his room.

Fortunately, Stephen's father received new orders shortly afterward and the family moved to a different house, free from lingering and troublesome spirits. Now an adult, Stephen has no doubt, even to this day, that his sister's innocent "playing around" with a Ouija board that afternoon in Germany resulted in their home becoming haunted. He had known it from the moment the shadow man crossed his path.

Buyer Beware

New, direct-from-the-factory Ouija boards are bad enough. But old, used ones are even worse. Who knows what arcane, or profane, rituals they were used for in the past? Or what part of the past decided to stay attached until it found a new host?

Shelly's father brought home a used Ouija board when she was fifteen. He often bought things at yard sales and thrift stores with the intention of polishing them up and re-selling them on eBay for a profit. This time, though, he thought Shelly and her sister, Patti, might like to play with the board and gave it to them as a gift. The girls thanked him but secretly had no interest in trying it out. They put it away in the garage and quickly forgot all about it.

About a week later strange things started happening. Shelly remembers "the trouble" beginning when she was awakened at exactly 3:03 a.m. one night. Though she couldn't remember having a nightmare or hearing anything out of the ordinary, she woke up feeling very agitated and frightened. Seeing Patti sleeping peacefully across the room they shared afforded her some comfort, and after a while she was able to fall back asleep herself. The next night Shelly awoke again at precisely 3:03. And again she felt scared out of her wits for some unknown reason. She tossed and turned for a time before finally settling her head down sideways. She was just about to nod off when a man's voice, clearly and directly, said into her ear, "Go back to sleep." Shelly jumped up and looked wildly around. No one else was in the room but her sleeping sister. Shelly cowered under the covers fully awake the rest of the night.

A few days later, Shelly was alone in the house watching a movie. Needing to go to the bathroom, she paused the player and left the room. When she returned, she was stunned to see the disc drive on the DVD player wide open, the DVD out of the player and lying next to the TV, and the living room in an absolute shambles.

Up to that point, Shelly had been the only witness to or victim of the strange events happening in the house. Until the day her sister let out a blood-curdling scream from the kitchen that even now Shelly will never forget. She and her father had been playing cards in the living room when Patti went into the kitchen for a drink. Upon hearing her scream, they raced into the kitchen and found Patti crouched on the floor, her back up against the stove. She was crying hysterically and had a look of shock on her face. When she finally calmed down enough to talk, she said she was about to open the refrigerator when she sensed there was someone behind her. She turned to look and that's when she screamed, for standing right in front of her was a dirty, bedraggled, white-haired old man . . . with no eyes. She turned to run but tripped instead. When she looked up the man was gone. Shelly and her father looked all around the kitchen, but the only way in or out—besides the way they had just entered—was through one door, and it was locked from the inside.

Shelly's father put the Ouija board for sale on eBay a few days later. He still wasn't convinced it had anything to do with the unexplained events reported by Shelly and Patti, even though the girls experienced no more frights after it had sold. One can only hope the new owners are as fortunate.

Uncle Aaron, Is That You?

Bella was only 12 when her uncle passed away unexpectedly from an undiagnosed heart condition. Her mother took his death very hard, and about a month afterward brought home a

Ouija board to try to contact him. Bella remembered sitting on the sofa while her mother, father, and grandma sat at a table, hunched over the board, their fingers splayed out on the plastic pointer while they asked the same questions over and over. "Aaron, can you hear us?" "Aaron, are you here?" As nothing interesting was happening, Bella was about to go watch television when suddenly her mother exclaimed, "It's moving!" Bella jumped up and watched in fascination as the planchette seemed to drag the adults' fingers around the board, resting briefly on a letter before jerkily moving to another one.

"Bella, grab a paper and pencil and write down these letters," instructed her mother. Bella did as she was told, and transcribed the letters her mother dictated to her. HELP ME, the letters spelled out. "Aaron? Aaron, how can we help you?" her mother asked. CANT LEAVE, came the reply. Bella remembered tears rolling down her mother's face as she tried to understand what her brother meant. She continued asking questions, but no other responses came that night. After about an hour, the family closed the board, still saddened but now also a bit confused.

That night around 3:00 a.m., Bella got up to use the bathroom. As she walked down the second-floor hallway back to her room, she was surprised to hear music coming from downstairs, especially as there weren't any lights on. Someone must have forgotten to turn the radio off, she thought as she continued toward her room. The next morning when she mentioned hearing the music in the middle of the night, her parents looked at her blankly. Neither of them had left the radio on, nor was it on when they woke up.

That evening Bella's mom and dad tried to reach Uncle Aaron again with the Ouija board. This time it didn't take long before they made contact. Bella's mother asked, "Are you okay?" The planchette moved to NO. "Why, Aaron? What's wrong?" she asked fervently. The planchette started moving wildly around the board, zipping from corner to corner. Finally, it slowed down and spelled out ITS COMING. "What's coming?" her mom and dad wanted to know. Suddenly the lights in the room started flickering. Bella's mom asked again, "What's coming?" The planchette moved back and forth before spelling out DEMON. At that very moment, an empty beer bottle next to Bella's dad shot straight up to the ceiling, making a hole in the plaster before falling back down and shattering on the floor. The petrified family quickly closed the board and left the room.

Bella was too frightened to sleep by herself that night, so she nestled in between her parents in their bedroom. She awoke again around 3:00 a.m., but not because she had to go to the bathroom. This time she was stirred awake by the sound of children outside the bedroom door. Giggling children. Terrified, she shook her mother, who answered, "Shh, I hear them too." They roused Bella's father, who groggily opened the door and announced there was no one there. "Go back to sleep. You're hearing things," he said as he fell back into bed. Bella and her mom didn't fall asleep for a long time, but thankfully they didn't hear or see anything else unusual either.

The next morning after breakfast, Bella's mom made a call to the local Catholic church and arranged for a priest to come out and bless the house. When Father Weitz arrived, the first thing he had Bella's mother do was get the Ouija board. He would take care of discarding it, he said, as sometimes people had trouble getting rid of them for good. Bella's mother looked at him quizzically and then went to retrieve the board. Just as she was handing it over to him, something made her cry out. To the amazement of everyone present, three slash marks appeared on her upper arm. After that, Father Weitz wasted no time in performing a blessing and a minor exorcism on the house. He also explained to the family that the "Aaron" they thought they were talking to was most likely a demon from the start, who was trying to gain their trust and sympathy so they would continue contacting it and thus grant it more power to cross into their realm.

With the Ouija board gone and the house blessed, Bella's family had no further trouble of a supernatural nature. Bella's mom came to accept that her brother Aaron was at peace, and with that decision she and the rest of her family were at peace too.

The Joker

One summer night in the year 2000, Marilee and three teenage friends tried out a Ouija board for the first time. Much to their delight, they conjured a spirit right away, who called itself "The Joker." The Joker seemed to be a friendly spirit who gave the girls accurate, and at times teasing, answers to their questions. When they asked him who he was when he was alive, he answered, ACTOR. When they asked how he died, he wrote, SICK.

Over the next couple of weeks, the girls got together regularly and chatted with The Joker. But by about the fourth session, the entity started changing its behavior. It would only answer questions spoken by Marilee, and at one point it told her they were meant to be together. Then there were the eerie events happening in the girls' homes, such as disembodied voices being heard and objects moving by themselves.

Determined to put an end to The Joker and his now unnerving and uninvited attention, the girls agreed to conduct one final Ouija board session where they commanded in the name of Jesus Christ that the spirit leave them alone. Then they closed the board and burned it in a backyard trash barrel. Thankfully, the strange phenomena in their houses stopped.

Several years later, curiosity got the better of Marilee and she decided to see if she could "find" The Joker again. But rather than use a Ouija board, this time she meditated until she received an answer that, yes, he was there. Marilee conversed with him in her mind for a while, until she felt the connection weaken and the presence leave. She felt they had parted on friendly terms and went to bed that night with no worries.

But a few hours later, she awoke to the sound of her cat hissing and growling. She looked toward where the cat was focusing its attention and saw a formless black shadow at the foot of her bed. Terror spread through her as she watched it grow bigger and rise up until it was hovering over her head. Remembering how she banished The Joker the first time, she immediately started praying out loud. In an instant, the shadow vanished and a sense of peace descended on the room. After that night,

Marilee renounced the practice of contacting spirits, and now only holds conversations with living, breathing human beings.

Phantom Footsteps

William's father had been an avid metaphysics enthusiast for nearly 50 years. So William wasn't too surprised to come home from work one evening to find an old Ouija board lying out on the kitchen table. Though he was an adult, William was temporarily living with his father, who was confined to a wheelchair and relied on William's assistance for some of his daily needs. This night, however, it appeared that his dad had gotten himself to bed, freeing William to relax on the couch with a snack in front of the television.

About ten minutes into his show, the kitchen light suddenly came on behind him with an audible click. William jumped, hesitated for a few minutes, and then got up to investigate. Walking into the kitchen, he saw nothing out of the ordinary. The back door was locked, nothing was out of place, and even the Ouija board was how he remembered it. Thinking it must have been an electrical glitch, William turned the light out, the television off, and went upstairs to his bedroom.

He hadn't been asleep for more than an hour when he was jolted awake by a terrifying sound—the clomp of heavy footsteps coming up the stairs toward his room. The sound was unmistakable, as the house was very old and creaky, its wood frame quick to amplify any little movement. The footsteps continued thudding right up to William's closed door and then abruptly stopped. Frozen with fear, William cowered under his covers, too afraid to look out and risk seeing a monstrosity staring back at him. He remained that way until his shakes finally gave way to sleep.

The next morning, William found no evidence that an intruder had been in the house. Nor had his father heard anything after he had gone to bed. William's thoughts immediately went to the Ouija board left out in the kitchen, and he demanded that his father throw it out. "It leaves or I do," warned William. His father obliged. As no other strange events occurred after that, the phantom intruder apparently left also.

This Little Piggy

It had been raining for three straight days, and 14-year-old Dylan and his friends were bored out of their minds. Life in their small Iowa town moved pretty slow on nice days, but the bad weather practically ground things to a halt. They decided to go to the local thrift store, as it was nearby and they had nothing better to do.

One of the boys spotted a Ouija board sitting on a shelf. It was in good condition, still in the original box, and even included the instructions. The boys didn't hesitate. They had just found their Friday night entertainment! They gathered back at Dylan's house and quickly went about setting up the board on a card table in the basement. After going over the instructions carefully, the three boys placed their fingers on the plastic planchette and took turns asking questions such as: "Are there any spirits here with us?" At one point, Dylan thought the planchette jerked on its own toward the word YES, but his buddies guffawed and said he was really the one moving it. After a half hour of asking increasingly silly questions and getting no responses, the boys gave up and resigned themselves to another night of watching reruns on television.

The following afternoon, Dylan's parents had errands to run, leaving Dylan at home by himself. At about 3:00 p.m, Dylan wandered out to the kitchen to get a bowl of cereal. As he sat at the table eating, he heard a buzzing sound. Thinking it was coming from one of the electrical appliances, he checked the kitchen thoroughly but couldn't find the source. He checked the other rooms to no avail, but strangely enough, the buzzing seemed to follow him from one end of the house to the other. He was about to grab his shoes and head outside to see if he could hear the sound out there when suddenly the nauseating odor of rotten meat overwhelmed him. He ran out the door in his socks and eagerly inhaled the fresh air. Grateful that neither the buzzing sound nor the foul odor had followed him, Dylan stayed on the front porch until his parents arrived home.

The rest of the day proved uneventful, and by the time Dylan went to bed, he had pretty much forgotten all thoughts of the bad meat smell and unexplained buzzing. He fell asleep fast and slept soundly until 3:00 a.m., when he awoke to a noise coming from outside his bedroom door. It sounded like a large animal was sniffing under the door. Dylan instantly came alert: his family didn't have any pets. As the sniffing grew louder and more insistent, Dylan found himself frozen in place with fear. But when the thing outside his door grunted like some sort of feral pig, Dylan found his voice and screamed for help. His parents ran into his room, and Dylan was shocked that they didn't see anything on their way in. The noises stopped too, and for a minute Dylan thought maybe he had imagined all of it.

But then the rotten meat smell descended. And the buzzing began. And Dylan could tell by the confused and frightened looks on his parents' faces that they were experiencing the same things. The three of them spent the rest of the night together in Dylan's parents' room, where they were able to sleep for a few hours after the sensory assaults finally ended.

The next morning, Dylan's parents arranged for a priest to come out to the house and bless it. Before he began, the priest asked if anyone in the family had recently brought anything new into the house—a statue, book, or artifact, perhaps? Dylan was hesitant to mention the Ouija board from the thrift store for fear his parents would get angry, but when the priest next asked if anyone had been involved in occult activities, Dylan couldn't keep quiet any longer. His fear of whatever was in the house was stronger than the fear of his parents' disapproval.

The priest gave the family a brief, but pointed, explanation of the dangers of the occult, especially Ouija boards. "You're not the first folks who have called me after playing around with one of those things," he said. After making Dylan promise he wouldn't touch a Ouija board again, the priest cleansed and blessed the house. Before leaving, he offered to take the board with him for proper disposal, which Dylan and his parents gratefully agreed to.

Thankfully, the ritual seemed to work, as Dylan's family didn't experience any further paranormal disturbances after that. And on rainy days, Dylan and his friends did what all the other teenagers in town did. They went to the mall.

A Call From Paul

In the 1960s, the Ouija board reached its peak in popularity, selling more units even than the venerable board game Monopoly. Meeting/event planner and writer Laurie Fellezs grew up in that era and remembers well her own experience with the "The Mystifying Oracle" that was all the rage back then. She remembers it vividly because it scared the hell out of her. And that idiom might be more appropriate than one thinks.

This is Laurie's story, as posted on Medium.com. She has graciously allowed it to be reprinted here.

I Messed With a Ouija Board

The Ouija Board fascinated my friends and me back in the sixth grade. We would play with it at slumber parties and during evenings when it was too cold to run around in the streets at night in suburban 1960s Santa Rosa. We were young, naïve, and it was something unusual and mysterious — a diversion to play when you didn't have hours to devote to Monopoly or Clue. We didn't know what could happen if you played with it. That is, until we called a spirit into my house.

I don't remember much in my childhood but I remember that whole experience. It scarred me for life.

My best friend, Joan, who lived across the street, and I were sitting in my dining room with the Ouija board between us. We were spending what seemed like hours asking it the typical questions young girls want answers to: "Did Ronnie like me?" "Were we going to have a boyfriend soon?" "Did any boy we know like us?" They were the typical all-important topics we pondered and fretted over on any given day.

Finally, we asked the "spirit" if it had a name. The plastic disk our fingers rested on began to move around as before, back and forth, and pausing before slowly spelled out a name: P-A-U-L.

We were delighted and mesmerized. Was there really a spirit at the other end?

After a few more questions and answers from Paul, we asked him where he was. After much moving around on the board, the disk slowly spelled out its answer: I-N, pause, Y-O-U-R, pause, B-E-D.

Screaming in terror and suddenly feeling something like foreboding sweep through the room, we immediately stopped playing the game and decided it was best to call it a night.

Though scared and creeped out at the time, I—being a typical 11-year-old girl—soon forgot about our brush with evil. That is, until one day a few months later.

At that time in my life, I loved to sleep in late whenever I could. It was not unusual for me to sleep until late morning while the rest of the household was awake and active.

This morning was no different and I remember I was slowly waking up to the sound of my mom in the backyard watering the garden. I was laying on my side with my back to the rest of my pink daisy wallpapered room. It was bright outside and the hot sun was streaming in through the white curtains. It was going to be a beautiful summer day.

Then I heard it.

It was heavy breathing in my right ear. It sounded like that obscene phone call from a horror film. You know, the kind of call the woman receives right before the murderer appears in the house. I was half asleep and my eyes were still closed as I tried to figure out whether I had been dreaming.

I awoke fully and lay still. It was there all right and I listened to it for a couple of minutes trying to figure out where it was coming from.

Then, I knew. It was my little brother, Russell, trying to scare me. He always got up early and thought it would be funny to wake me up and scare me in the process.

Well, I was smarter than him. I was going to scare him.

I waited another couple of seconds, patiently listening to his breathing. Then, I flipped over, tossing my covers back, and screamed out at him, "AWWWWWWWW!"

The room was empty.

I never played with the Ouija Board again.

* * *

For more of Laurie's essays and travel adventures, visit her on Medium and at LaurieFellezs.com.

Chapter 6

Fiendish Attacks

"They are vile creatures of the night. And they are among us in many instances solely because of these sinister toys called Ouija boards."

– Dr. Alberto Gonzalez, psychiatrist and parapsychologist

Terror in Wales

In 2015, a South Wales couple made headlines in the British tabloids with their sensational story of being under attack by demons after a relative used a Ouija board in their house. Their frightening narrative was perfect tabloid fodder, but their insistence and sincerity also convinced a paranormal investigator and a Church of Wales clergyman to try to help the terror-stricken family.

According to father-of-three Keiron Fry, the trouble started after his stepson played with a Ouija board in their house the previous Halloween and used it to deliberately invoke demons. In the months that followed, Keiron and his wife, Tracey, would wake in the morning to find themselves battered and bruised—but without any memory of an attack happening.

"My wife goes to bed fine, doesn't feel anything in the night but when she wakes up she's in agony. I wake up the next day and said: 'I didn't do that.' I would never beat my wife."

Tracey has borne the brunt of the attacks. Photographs provided to Wales News Service show large red welts on her back that she says continuously hurt no matter how much cream Keiron rubs on them. These physical assaults, as well as other strange poltergeist-like activity like objects moving on their own, kept the family feeling like they were prisoners in their own house. Even the cats became afraid to go upstairs, where the paranormal activity seemed most intense.

But it was when the Frys' children heard a demonic voice say, "I'm going to slit your parents' throats," that the couple decided they needed professional help. They called paranormal investigator and psychic medium Robert Amour to come out and do a "house cleansing," hoping the veteran ghostbuster with over 20 years of experience dealing with supernatural entities could drive out whatever had taken up residence in their home. Arriving at the Frys' house armed with a Bible and a crucifix, Amour immediately sensed "an evilness" coming from the second floor. He instructed the Frys to remain where they were while he went upstairs and conducted a 20-minute exorcism.

When he came back down, Amour had bad news and good news for the anxious couple. The bad news was that the Frys didn't just have one spirit haunting them—they had three. And one of them was an incubus, a particularly bad demon that attacks women in their sleep, often sexually, and hence the physical assaults on Tracey. The good news was that Amour believed he had successfully driven the demons out.

Despite Amour's assurances, Keiron reported later that at least one entity was still in the house, as the attacks on Tracey and other disturbing phenomena were still occurring. "It has affected our marriage because we have been rowing and fighting all the time about the demon. It has been feeding off all the negative energy."

Church of Wales Vicar Jonathan Widdess has also visited the Frys in an effort to rid them of their evil spirit. "We spoke about what was going on. We said a prayer to try and help him," recalled Widdess.

The Frys have shied away from the public eye in recent years, so it is unknown if they continue to be oppressed by demonic entities. Robert Armour has remained firm in his belief that "the spirits that were troubling them had been cleansed," but has nonetheless extended an invitation for the Frys to get in touch with him if they felt the need.

"Quite honestly there is a lot of this going on," Amour said in an interview with *WalesOnline*, referring to reports of malevolent spirits. "My workload is high now and one thing I'd urge people is not to use Ouija boards."

Not surprisingly, the Frys are no longer on speaking terms with the relative who started all their trouble with one such demon-summoning board.

Challenge Accepted

It was an invitation Luke Jackson couldn't turn down. The South Yorkshire Ghost Hunters club was holding their weekly Thursday night meeting at the Monkwood Pub near Rotherham, where they regularly invited members of the public to join them. Luke, while skeptical of things like ghosts and demons, was still curious enough to attend the session. If nothing else, there was ale to be had.

The ghost hunters had their equipment set up and their stations manned when Luke arrived. Several members were gathered around a small circular "tippy table," their fingers gently resting on the outer edges of the table, ready to detect the actions of playful ghosts, while another group was situated around a Ouija board and attempting to open a portal to the spirit world. On a third table sat an electromagnetic field detector, there for the purpose of alerting the participants to the presence of ethereal, energy-guzzling beings. According to Luke, the night started out low-key, with people milling about back and forth between the tables, curious but behaving themselves. Suddenly the lights on the EMF detector started flickering, low intermittent pulses of yellow light at first, but soon reaching the highest level, red, at a continuous rate.

The lead questioner at the Ouija board asked if a spirit was present. The planchette started moving around the board. At the same time, the tippy table began turning counterclockwise. The ghost hunters tried to get the spirit to tell them who it was, but as suddenly as all the activity started, it stopped. Except for the EMF detector. It continued to show a high reading.

It was at this point that Luke, who had been walking around and watching everything with a skeptical eye, barked out a verbal challenge: "If you have so much power, do something that will show us that you are definitely here."

The response was swift—and severe.

Instantly after issuing his challenge, Luke felt what he described as "three pins" scrape down his back. He lifted his shirt and there in plain sight of the gathered crowd were three fresh-looking scratch marks, about six inches each in length. "Bloody hell!" Luke exclaimed. Though the scratches weren't deep and didn't require medical attention, their traumatic appearance upset Luke more than he wanted to admit. "I went outside and had a fag and a pint to calm down after the whole ordeal," Luke recalled. Before the night was over, another member of the group was scratched on her neck and the top of her back.

Many people would have been hesitant to return after an encounter like Luke's, but not only did he rejoin the ghost hunters for the rest of the evening, he has since become a regular member of their group and meets with them weekly. "I've always been skeptical and I was a skeptic up until that point and I've always tried to disbelieve and disprove—but after that night in February my view has changed completely."

Luke has learned his lesson, though, about offering challenges to the spirits. As he found out the hard way, they're more than willing to accept them.

Scary Sarah

Irene and her teenage friends often played with a Ouija board when they got together for sleepovers. They would ask innocuous questions like who would they marry, how many children would they have, and so forth. For them, it was like playing with a Magic 8 Ball. Nothing bad ever happened. In fact, nothing ever happened at all, except lots of giggling and melodramatic acting when the planchette "moved" under their practiced fingers. All in all, Irene considered it just harmless fun.

The friends eventually lost their interest in the Ouija as they got older. They went their separate ways after high school, forged new relationships, and pursued different passions. But one night while Irene was away at college, she spotted a Ouija board in her dormitory's common room and was instantly flooded with fond memories of playing with the board. As there wasn't anything else to do that night, Irene convinced her dormmates to join her in trying it out. It wasn't long before the group contacted a spirit that called itself Sarah. The girls took turns asking Sarah silly questions, which, to their delight, Sarah answered amenably. They ended their session after a few hours, as they had classes early the next morning. But the girls all agreed to meet again soon to "chat" with Sarah some more.

The dormmates did indeed continue to use the Ouija, but as Irene later recalled, it was as if they were becoming "entrapped" by the board and were compelled by some unknown force to use it as often as possible. One night as they gathered to play, a new girl from the floor above, Kristen, joined them. As usual, the group contacted Sarah within minutes. But this time, the questions and answers had a decidedly different tone.

"We started asking Sarah how she died, how old she was when she died, and finally what she looked like," Irene said.

Sarah told them she died at age 23 when a runaway horse and carriage hit her. When the co-eds asked what she looked like, Sarah spelled out LIKE KRIS BLUE EYES. One of the girls asked Sarah to show them what she meant. Sarah then spelled out LOOK AT KRIS. The girls stared at Kristen, who was a bit uncomfortable at this point, and gasped as they watched her green eyes suddenly turn blue and her facial features become more angular. Kristen screamed, and just as suddenly as it occurred, the transformation reversed, leaving Kristen looking like herself again, only visibly shaken and pale. She said it felt as if an electric current had run through her.

One of the girls started to get up to get Kristen a glass of water, but she didn't get far before letting out an ear-piercing shriek. "Look! In the window!" The others turned and saw what appeared to be a head looking in on them from the window—a window that was three stories up from the ground.

Irene immediately refocused on the Ouija board and asked, "Are you Sarah?" The planchette moved to NO. "Who are you then?" she asked. The planchette started spelling out SATA . . . but the girls didn't let it finish. They had had enough. Irene knocked the planchette off the board and told everyone to go back to their rooms. The figure in the window had vanished, but in its wake a sudden coldness descended on the room, so cold in fact the girls could see their breath.

"We were so frightened that none of us could sleep," recalled Irene. They decided to spend the night in the room next to Irene's, thinking they could listen for anything out of the ordinary. At around 2:30 a.m., they ventured out for a snack to a vending machine in the hall. As they passed Irene's room, they heard an alarm clock go off, an alarm that had been set for 6:30. They decided they would go in as a group to turn off the alarm; when they opened the door they were aghast to see all the windows thrown open and the sheets pulled off the beds.

As Irene's roommate, Sandy, bent down to turn the clock off, the two necklaces she was wearing started to twist around each other. Choking as the necklaces squeezed tighter around her neck, Sandy fled from the room and ripped them off. That's when she noticed that a cross pendant from one of them had moved to the other chain.

The girls knew without a doubt they were dealing with forces beyond their control. Being Catholic, they contacted the campus priest first thing the next morning and told him everything that had happened. The priest came to Irene's room, blessed it with holy water, and then took the Ouija board out and burned it. Before he left, he gave the girls a stern lecture on the dangers of dabbling in the occult. Even if he hadn't, Irene and her friends would never be persuaded to touch a Ouija board or anything like it ever again. The next week, Irene requested, and was granted, a new dorm room.

Demonic Rapists

Sightings was a popular paranormal news television show in the 1990s. Several of its episodes featured Ouija board stories, but perhaps the most disturbing narrative came from an anonymous female user who reported the following terrifying incident:

"When I first started using the Ouija board it was just for fun. And then, about a year ago, I took it out and something happened, and I got scared, and I put it away. And I went to bed. It was about 1:00, 1:30, and I kept feeling like there was something or someone in the room. And, I tried to get up, and I was pushed down. This tremendous force on my chest was picking me up and throwing me back down again. I felt like I was being attacked. I grabbed the sheets and tried to hold down to the bed, but I couldn't. I felt like I was being raped."

It's likely this narrator was the victim of an incubus, a demon that sexually assaults women. A succubus is its counterpart entity, an evil spirit that forces itself sexually on a man. Famed demonologist and paranormal investigator Ed Warren (now deceased) dealt with many incubus attacks during his working years, seventy-five percent of which, he estimated, were the consequence of unwitting use of a Ouija board. "The Ouija board opens the doors to the supernatural, to supernatural attack," Ed warned. "When you use the Ouija board, you're communicating with an invisible, intangible realm, and negative spirits can enter through the board."

One such case Ed recalled involved a 28-year-old Colorado

woman who was a frequent user of the Ouija, as well as a Tarot card reader and psychic. Despite her knowledge and experience with the occult, she made "the devastating mistake," as she called it, of trying to contact her recently deceased mother through the Ouija board. She wrote to Ed: "I got results, but it was not my mother whom I contacted. It was some sort of entity which had watched me since her death. I don't know what it is, but I know it is not human."

In the course of the lengthy letter she sent to Ed, she detailed the horrific physical, mental, and verbal abuse she endured for several years. "Every day it viciously rapes, sodomizes and beats me . . . When it was done with me that first time, I needed medical care for the pain and for pelvic and bladder infections."

The demon did all it could to drive the young woman to take her own life, a favorite tactic of its kind. "It does all it can to force me to commit suicide! Constant badgering and berating," she wrote. "Verbal abuse so foul and sickening and dirty it is unbelievable . . . My husband often finds me on the floor or hiding or screaming so loud I'm afraid I might be carted out!"

In her letter she also sheds light on an intriguing yet horrifying ploy the demon used while attacking her. "It calls itself Sheikh Abdullah and speaks in a heavy Arabic accent. It has pretended to be many people and can make a voice like my mother's. It creates illusions and terrible, terrible visions, anything ugly it can add while it rapes and beats me."

Ed, and his wife Lorraine, herself a psychic sensitive, did

eventually help this poor woman escape the clutches of her demonic torturer. It was not without great effort, however, and the risk of re-occurrence if she ever ventured back to her previous occult practices.

> *"If that person, for whatever reason, decides they want to mess with a Ouija board again, or delve into any form of occult, that's dangerous. They're opening themselves right back up, and those demons will come right back inside."*
>
> **– Most Rev. Dr. Isaac Kramer, exorcist**

The Slapper

With nothing better to do one dreary Saturday afternoon, Ron and several friends dug out an old Ouija board and decided to have a séance. As there were no parents home, the teenagers made the living room as spooky as they could to enhance the mood. They closed the curtains, lit candles, and even hung up some Halloween decorations they found in the basement. Then they began, with Ron and three others placing their fingers on the plastic planchette and taking turns asking questions. Nothing much was happening, so Ron decided he'd make things more interesting by challenging the "spirits" to be physical with him.

"If you're here, tap my shoulder," he demanded. "Squeeze my neck." The others were getting nervous by Ron's brashness, but he continued. "Prove yourself! Give me a push." Suddenly Ron's back began to sting. "Hey!" he yelled, jumping up from the table. He lifted his shirt and there, to the horror of everyone present, were three handprints impressed on his back, red and puffy like he'd just been slapped. After that, Ron didn't feel the need to offer any more challenges. Nor did he ever play around with a Ouija board again.

Evil Moves In

Like many first encounters with a Ouija board, Karina's and Liza's started off as simple curiosity. Did it really work? The friends decided to find out for themselves after Karina brought home a used board from a thrift shop. She and Liza set it up on a table in Karina's living room, read the instructions, and started to play. For the first half of the session, nothing much happened. The planchette moved a little when they inquired about deceased relatives, but nothing occurred that convinced them the Ouija was "the real deal."

They were about to give up when two of their friends came bursting into the room, laughing and joking. The Ouija board, of course, caught their eye and they immediately wanted to join the game. Once everyone had quieted down, the foursome placed their fingers on the planchette and restarted the session. Karina had barely asked the first question when the plastic pointer started moving frantically under their touch. At first it spelled out random names but then changed to a more disturbing tone with words like LUST and MURDER. Any joviality the group had been feeling a short time earlier had quickly dissipated; no one argued when Karina announced, "That's it," and packed the board away.

A few days later, Karina started waking up at 3:00 a.m. every night with an unexplainable feeling of dread. She told a friend about this one night while walking back home together after a party. As the two turned to go down a dimly lit street near Karina's house, she was startled to see a black figure leaning on a fence staring at them. Her friend saw it too, but only for an instant before it vanished into the shadows. Nervously, they joked about the street being haunted while quickening their steps toward home.

That night, Karina was awakened by the terrifying sensation of a man pinning her face down on the bed. As she struggled to scream—to breathe, even—the man whispered coarsely in her ear but she couldn't understand what he was saying. Then suddenly the weight lifted and the presence disappeared. Karina was too afraid to do anything other than burrow under her covers until sleep mercifully overcame her.

A few days later, Karina's grandmother, who was known among family and friends to possess psychic sensitivity, visited the home. As soon as she walked in, she said she felt a presence in the house, a negative presence. Karina's mom chimed in that she, too, had felt something "different" in the house over the last week. Suspecting that her Ouija board might be to blame, Karina told her mom and grandma about how she and her friends had experimented with it recently. Karina's mom didn't seem to think that in itself was any big deal, but her grandmother strongly disagreed. "Get rid of it. It's evil!" warned her grandmother.

As Karina's mom and grandma began arguing over the Ouija

board, a strange sensation overcame Karina. It was the same feeling of dread she had awakened to all those nights at 3:00 a.m. But it was stronger and it was accompanied by another sensation—one of being pulled into a tunnel further and further away from the room she was in. She began to panic as she became unable to speak or move. Finally, with great effort, she screamed: "There's something wrong with me!" The next thing she knew, her sister, mom, and grandma were at her side, embracing and comforting her. They told her it looked as if she had had a seizure.

The very next day, the family arranged for a priest to come over and bless the house. As he went through the rooms reading his prayers, all the pipes in the house made a loud screeching noise, as if adding a melodramatic flourish to the departure of whatever dark energies were present. When he was done, the priest took the Ouija board with him, promising to dispose of it properly. He didn't have to remind Karina not to fool around with one again. After that day, the family experienced peace in their household, but the memory of that dark period still scares Karina to this day.

The Bible Hater

Minister Tony Whitman was concerned about his sister, Debra, who for the past several months had been delving into the occult and showing signs of becoming obsessed with its practices. She had increasingly isolated herself from family and friends, and when Tony did see her, he noticed her personality had changed from congenial and warm to surly and cold.

Fearing for both her mental and spiritual safety, Tony decided it was time to confront Debra and convince her that she was endangering herself and hurting those who cared for her.

Tony's plan got off to a rocky start when he and his wife, Louise, showed up at Debra's house right as she was in the middle of a Ouija board session. Tony warned his sister that the board was devilish. Debra just laughed and invited Tony to show her exactly what he meant. Tony agreed but started to regret his decision almost immediately when a wave of depression and nausea rolled over him. He shook it off as best he could and sat down across from Debra at the Ouija table.

"Who are you?" Tony asked the entity Debra claimed was present.

SPIRIT, came the reply.

"What is your name?"

The planchette remained still. Tony's ministerial nature came forth and he asked, "Were you there at the resurrection of Christ?"

The entity answered, YES.

"What did you experience?"

FEAR.

Tony was starting to experience a bit of fear himself by this point, but he asked anyway, "What do you feel about me?"

HATE.

"What do you think about the Bible?"

The board spelled out an obscenity.

Tony looked up at his sister, hoping to see some sign of revulsion on her face, but saw only a blank expression. Disgusted and angry, he got up and announced he was done with the "demonic" board and then he threw his Bible on top of it.

Instantly the board levitated off the table and flung the Bible off with such force it hit the wall on the other side of the room. Debra and Louise screamed. Tony stared in disbelief, until a moment later when something slammed into his stomach, doubling him over and leaving him gasping for breath. The women ran over to help, and when they pulled up his shirt to examine him, they were aghast to see a fist-sized red welt on his midsection.

Debra, who at first suspected Tony was faking his injury, was now convinced that not only was the attack on Tony real, but that the Ouija board was indeed evil, as Tony had warned. The three of them grasped hands and recited a prayer of deliverance, after which they broke and burned the Ouija board.

Debra returned to her Christian faith, and Tony rejoiced that, by the grace of God, he had won his sister back from the dark side. Even if he had to take a punch in the gut to do it.

Chapter 7

Oppressions and Obsessions

"Quite often the Ouija turns vulgar, abusive or threatening. It grows demanding and hostile, and sitters may find themselves using the board compulsively, as if 'possessed' by a spirit, or hearing voices that control or command them."

– Martin Ebon, parapsychologist and author

The Price of Knowledge

Instead of their usual Friday night date of dinner and a movie, Scott and his girlfriend, Darcy, decided this time to stay in and play around with an old Ouija board Darcy had picked up at a yard sale. They dimmed the lights in Darcy's studio apartment, lit a couple of candles, and sat across from each other at a small table, the Ouija board between them. Darcy began by asking, "Are there any spirits here?" Scott, a self-described skeptic, really wasn't expecting anything to happen. So when the planchette started gliding around the board, he was at first surprised, then a bit suspicious. Was Darcy moving the pointer? She swore to him she wasn't. "Okay, then, let's ask our visitor some questions," said Scott.

As it turned out, their "ghost" (that's what Scott called it in his account of the experience) loved questions and answers, so much so that it engaged with the couple for seven hours. Darcy couldn't keep her eyes open any longer, excused herself from the conversation, and instantly fell asleep on the couch. Scott, on the other hand, didn't want to stop. He continued asking questions, but silently, in his head, so as to not wake up Darcy. To his amazement, he still received answers, even without Darcy's fingers on the planchette.

For several more hours, Scott continued to tap into this newly acquired font of knowledge (as addicting, he later stated, as any drug). When he caught a glimpse of the sun rising through the window blinds, he finally forced himself to get up and go home. Unfortunately, his new ghost friend decided to tag along.

"The ghost wouldn't leave me alone. It was always pestering me, wanting me to ask it more questions. Lights would flicker around me; I was seeing floating balls of different colors, and hearing loud noises no one else was."

Scott reached his breaking point with this spirit when it actually started moving parts of his body without his consent. He called a friend who was knowledgeable about the occult and explained what had been happening. His friend wasted no time. In a loud voice right over the phone, he commanded the spirit to "go to the light of Jesus Christ." To Scott's relief, the nonstop babbling inside his head, the flickering lights, and the loud noises stopped. The ghost was gone.

Within a few days, however, it became apparent to Scott that a

Ouija Board Nightmares 2

new spirit had attached itself to him—and this one was definitely worse. Not only did it also commandeer parts of his body, but it spoke through him. In a deep, growling voice, it called itself "the god of war" and said it wanted to kill people, including Scott. Then it told Scott that if he worshiped Satan he could have anything he wanted. Horrified, Scott invoked the name of Jesus for help, which he said made the spirit "go crazy" inside him. This gave Scott some means of managing his tormentor, but complete deliverance was yet to be found.

Unfortunately, as of this writing, Scott still suffers at the hand of his demonic oppressor. On a daily basis it makes different areas of his body twitch and spasm, and he is forced to listen to its vulgar and threatening diatribe inside his head. He has managed somehow to keep it from using his vocal chords anymore, but the constant struggle has exhausted him to the point of near despair. He made his story public to "scare straight" anyone thinking about playing around with a Ouija board. The answers it may provide, the curiosity it may assuage, aren't worth the nightmares and torture it could bring into your life. Scott admits he learned this the hard way, and his message remains firm: " Knowledge has a price."

Demonic Download

Patricia Quispe found out the hard way that there are worse things you can download than a virus. In 2015, the 18-year-old teen from Chosica, Peru, attended a party at which her friends were doing what most teens do these days when hanging out together: playing with their phones. Only this time, they were obsessed with a new app that they encouraged Patricia to download and try out with them. It was a Ouija board app, a 21st-century hi-tech version of the classic spirit board. Functioning basically the same as a physical Ouija, the app promised to serve as a conduit to the spirit world from which you would receive answers to your questions. The app was a huge success, keeping the teens entertained for hours until the party broke up.

After Patricia got home, she told her parents she wasn't feeling well and was going to bed. Several hours later, her parents were awakened by screams coming from their daughter's bedroom. They rushed in and were horrified to see Patricia convulsing and foaming at the mouth. They called paramedics, who spent a half hour trying to restrain the violently thrashing teen who was yelling, "666!" and "Let me go!" When the medics asked if the girl had taken any drugs or perhaps eaten something with hallucinogenic properties, the parents contacted her friends from the party, who confessed no to the drugs but yes to playing around with the Ouija app.

At the hospital, Patricia continued to convulse wildly while screaming obscenities and calling out for the devil. At one point, her voice changed so radically that several of the attending nurses and doctors stepped back and crossed themselves. After being thoroughly examined and tested for alcohol, drugs, or other foreign substances, doctors had no choice but to commit the still highly distressed and agitated teen to the psychiatric ward for further evaluation. Whispered rumors that an exorcist had been called were reported, but nothing official was ever released.

The Prodigal Sons

Lucas was the epitome of the All-American boy. Not only was he handsome, athletic, and popular, but he was also active in his church and attended classes at a Christian college along with his two best friends, Jake and Riley. To this day, Lucas isn't sure what spurred him to veer so wildly off his "good guy" path into the realm of the occult, but it was an experience that taught him a lesson for life.

While browsing at a second-hand shop, Lucas spotted a boxed Ouija board on a shelf with other board games. *Why not?* he thought to himself. He brought it home and convinced Jake and Riley to come over and try it out. The boys weren't sure what to expect but were thoroughly stoked by the anticipation of the unknown mixed with the spark of rebellion.

They set the board up on a table, lit some candles, and darkened the room. Then they figured if they were going to summon a spirit, they might as well go big: "May we have Satan in our presence," Lucas intoned. He no sooner stopped speaking when the planchette spun in a circle and flew off the table. The boys gasped but were determined to go on. "Is Satan here?" they asked. YES, came the reply. They asked several more questions about people and events they knew. The answers were eerily accurate, making the boys more uncomfortable by the minute. They were getting ready to say goodbye when suddenly the room became shockingly cold and the candles blew out by themselves. A feeling of evil descended on the room.

Terrified, the boys reverted to their religious beliefs. Riley threw a copy of the New Testament on the board, only to watch it scuttle off the table like a paperback crab. The boys began praying loudly, ordering the evil presence to leave, but to no avail. Not knowing what else to do, they left the house and headed off in Lucas' Jeep. Still not able to shake the feeling that they were in the midst of evil, the boys stopped at the nearest neighborhood church and prayed on the front lawn. Hours later, when they finally felt "alone," they returned to their homes and tried to put the terrifying events of the day behind them.

Unfortunately, whatever dark force pursued them that night was not gone for good, and it was soon apparent that it had made its mark on its intended targets. Lucas began to question his faith, while Jake and Riley stopped attending church completely. After several weeks, Jake started displaying severe and distressing personality traits—scathing anger, extreme anxiety, and overall brutish behavior toward everyone. Lucas suspected these changes were tied to their Ouija board experience, and he sought the help of his religious studies professor to figure out what to do about it. His professor advised him to renounce all connection to the occult, destroy the Ouija board, and pray to God for deliverance from the occult spirit that held Lucas and his friends in its power.

Lucas headed home with the firm intention to carry out these instructions, even as he was bombarded with voices inside his head warning him not to destroy the board. They were the same voices he had heard after returning home the night of the Ouija debacle. He had wanted to throw the board away then, but instead he gave in to the voices telling him to pack it away in a closet. This time, though, he ignored the voices and broke and burned the board as soon as he arrived at his house. Then he vomited violently, as wave after wave of nausea overtook him. Thankfully, it passed quickly, and soon a renewed feeling of faith — and victory — settled over him.

The next Sunday, Lucas was surprised to see his friend Riley at the 10:00 service. Riley told him that it was kind of strange, but he found himself thinking about going back to church on Friday — the very Friday that Lucas destroyed the Ouija board. It took Jake a bit longer to come back, but eventually he did too, with no trace of the brutish alter ego that had bedeviled him earlier.

Mom's Obsession

Frank was nineteen when he decided to take a year out of his studies and do some traveling. In letters and telephone calls with his older brothers and sisters, he had learned, among other things, that his mom had picked up a new hobby: using a Ouija board. This didn't surprise Frank too much, as his mom had always had an interest in the New Age and had an extensive library on topics such as channeling, crystals, and reincarnation.

In the days right before he returned home, though, his siblings gave him a rather disturbing warning. Mom had changed, they told him. She's wasn't the same. So when Frank showed up at his family home, he expected to see that his mom had perhaps put on some weight or had dyed her hair. But when his mom greeted him at the door, she looked pretty much like he remembered her. On the outside, at least. It was when she put her hands on his shoulders, looked him directly in the eye, and said in a low voice, "Welcome home, Frank," that chills ran through his body. The woman in front of him was a stranger. There was a *repulsiveness* about her that he couldn't explain, but it impelled him to squirm out of her grip and awkwardly return her greeting.

After exchanging news and pleasantries with his other relatives, Frank retired to his bedroom for a nap. Maybe his mom just seemed strange to him because he was overtired from his trip, he told himself. He quickly fell asleep but was awakened a few hours later by a feeling of being watched. He opened his eyes and gave a start when he saw his mom standing directly over him, staring at him with black, vacant eyes while smoking a cigarette. Frank couldn't remember his mom ever smoking in the house, to say nothing about in his bedroom. His mom muttered something about checking to see if he needed anything, then left without another word.

Later that night, as Frank was reading in his room, he heard what he thought was a party going on downstairs. Thinking that his parents had invited some people over, he went downstairs prepared to see a crowd. But what he saw instead was just a solitary figure—his mother—hunched over a Ouija board and talking in a variety of voices, male and female. Under her fingertips the plastic planchette was moving crazily; whether guided by his mother or by forces unknown, Frank couldn't be sure. He called out to his mom. She whipped her head in his direction and hissed at him, "Go away!" The scene in front of him too surreal to deal with at that moment, Frank backed out of the room.

The next morning, he told his father about the nightmarish episode, but to his dismay his father just shrugged and told Frank not to worry about it. "It's your mother's hobby. It makes her happy." But Frank wasn't convinced. His mother definitely did not look happy last night. She looked distressed, as if other *things* were taking up residence in her body and using her. Later that day, Frank confronted his mother about the Ouija board. A heated argument followed, resulting in Frank taking the board out and burning it. His mom went out and bought a new board later that day.

Frank knew at that point there wasn't much he could do to separate his mom from her Ouija board obsession. He did his best to make peace with her, and shortly thereafter moved out into his own apartment. He got used to his mom's new "strangeness," always reminding himself that somewhere under the layers was the woman he remembered from his childhood. He never lost hope that someday she would find the strength to re-emerge. But unfortunately his mom stayed attached to her Ouija board until the day she died. As much as Frank would like to know she's okay and at peace, he won't succumb to the temptation to use a Ouija to find out. He knows firsthand how it can take over people's lives.

The Sleepover from Hell

Seventeen-year-old Miranda Huberty was an avid student of the paranormal and occult, and the Ouija board was her favorite means of exploring the preternatural realm. After months of practicing, Miranda was ecstatic when one night she actually made contact with what she believed to be a friendly spirit. The entity told Miranda he used to work on the nearby docks many years ago. When Miranda asked how he died, the spirit replied, DROWNED. After a little while it became apparent the spirit was no longer is a chatty mood, and Miranda got up to put the board away in her closet. She was startled, however, by an unnerving feeling of being followed by something dark and willowy, like a shadow but with malicious intent. As nothing out of the ordinary was visible, she shrugged it off as best she could and went to bed.

The next day at school, Miranda found it difficult to concentrate in her classes, as she was bombarded by a constant stream of strange and vulgar thoughts and fantasies. When she got home she was so exhausted by fighting off the unwanted images in her head that she took a three-hour nap, only to be awakened by that same feeling of a dark presence nearby. She ate a late dinner, did some homework, and then fell back into bed, where she didn't stir until morning.

Refreshed from a good night's sleep, Miranda was brushing her teeth and feeling optimistic about the upcoming day when suddenly the bathroom mirror started to "come alive" with moving images. She stared in amazement as before her a movie scene played out in which her boyfriend, Nick, got into a fender-bender with another student on the way to school. Then as quickly and mysteriously as it came, the picture vanished, leaving Miranda staring at her own pale, bewildered face. As soon as she arrived at school and saw that Nick wasn't there, she knew what she had seen was real. By mid-morning, news of the non-injurious accident was confirmed.

That night, while getting ready for bed, Miranda looked into the bathroom mirror and froze with fear when she saw another face behind her own, just to the left of her shoulder. A grotesque distortion of herself, this face had dark rings around the eyes, a greenish complexion, and stringy hair. When its mouth formed into an evil leer, Miranda shrieked, dropped to her knees and urgently prayed for protection from any and all evil spirits. When she finally got up and looked, the mirror was clear.

The next day at school, Miranda decided to tell her three best friends—Jo, Kari, and Annette— what was going on. Like Miranda, the other three girls had an intense interest in the occult and were mesmerized by Miranda's account of the shadow presence, the troubling fantasies, and the mirror images that all happened after Miranda's Ouija board "contact." They were so interested, in fact, that they suggested another Ouija board session to see if they could identify the entity that had been bothering Miranda. Despite her initial reluctance, Miranda agreed to get together on Friday night for a slumber party séance.

As the hour approached midnight on Friday, the four friends along with Miranda's 12-year-old sister, Dani, gathered around the Ouija, placed their fingers on the planchette, and began "summoning." To their delight, it wasn't long before a spirit calling itself Suzanne answered their call. Suzanne said she was a seamstress from the 1880s who had been killed by runaway horses. She remained earthbound for many years after her death because her paramour, Jonathan, had still loved her so strongly. Just as the girls were getting teary-eyed from this story of sweet, eternal love, Suzanne suddenly bombarded them with lewd descriptions of the sexual activities she and Jonathan engaged in, both before and after her death. Then she told the girls that they too could have lovers from beyond the grave.

Repulsed, the girls pulled their hands away from the board. Miranda was about to declare an end to the session when all of a sudden Annette dropped to the floor and started twitching spasmodically. When the other girls knelt down to help her, Annette sat up and leered at them with a maniacal grin on her face. Then she spewed obscenities at them while looking wildly around until she locked eyes with Dani. Like a feral animal, Annette pounced on the twelve-year-old and tried to forcibly kiss her on the mouth. Miranda pulled Annette away from her sister and then watched in horror as the image of another woman—a horribly ugly and bent hag—superimposed itself over Annette. Jo grabbed a religious icon she wore around her neck, held it at arm's length and shouted, "Begone, evil demon! Leave us alone!" Annette jumped on Jo, knocked her to the ground and began strangling her with her bare hands.

The shouts and thuds brought Miranda's parents rushing into the room, where they beheld a vision of mass chaos: screaming girls tussling with one another and objects tossed about like an earthquake had hit. More annoyed at first than alarmed, Miranda's dad shouted over the noise that the party was over and he would be driving the girls home. But when normally polite-to-a-fault Annette whipped her head around, spat in his face, and cursed at him in a chilling, guttural voice, it became clear that this wasn't a typical teenage squabble.

"Dad, there's something in her! We have to do something," Miranda pleaded. Miranda's dad had everyone join hands to form a circle around Annette, and as a group they started to pray. Annette became even more incensed, dropped to the ground and began hissing and growling. Dani screamed and ran to her mother, who carried her out of the room. The others continued their prayer, and after a few minutes a blessed silence fell over the group. Several more minutes passed before Annette sat up, blinked, and asked—in her regular voice— what had happened. Because it was the middle of the night, and since things seemed back to normal, Miranda's parents decided to keep the girls at their house for the rest of the night.

After Miranda's friends left the next morning (Annette still had no recollection of her strange behavior the night before), Miranda's parents had a heart-to-heart talk with her about her occult activities. While they had never forbidden her to pursue her hobby, they weren't crazy about it either. Last night's hysteria was an example of why. Miranda then told them about the dark entity that she believed attached itself to her after her Ouija board sessions, and about the disturbing thoughts and visions she had experienced. After more honest conversation, the family decided that it was best for Miranda—and for those around her who could be affected—to set aside her paranormal pursuits for the foreseeable future. A future not foretold by a Ouija board.

Miranda's family experienced no further paranormal disturbances after that chaotic sleepover. An investigator they spoke to later about the case advised them that a combination of their earnest prayers that night and Miranda's promise to give up her occult activities had most likely restored a balance of positive energy both in the home and in Miranda's ongoing personal development.

Warning from a Demonologist

Gavin Canavan, a demonologist from Ireland, believes the proliferation of paranormal reality shows on television has contributed in large part to the upsurge of people getting themselves in trouble with Ouija boards. Many times on these shows, the "ghost hunters" are shown using the boards during the course of their investigations, with the disclaimer that they are professionals and know what they're doing. At other times, these reality stars, both on television or on social media, will use Ouija boards at public events or on streaming specials to generate ratings, likes, and followers. Canavan thinks this is a bad idea.

"I personally would not agree with paranormal groups using Ouija boards as entertainment. Sure, they may do a live feed using a Ouija board and may not get feedback that night, but that does not mean they will be that lucky again.

"These groups do not tell people to use them but treat them as a toy and make people believe they are safe to use. In my experience, things can happen, and I have witnessed the devastating lasting effects on the people who have used them."

Canavan has witnessed a lot. In his career as a demonologist, during which he has visited hundreds of homes suspected of being "haunted" or infested by demonic spirits, he has been kicked, punched, and growled at by entities that are usually invisible to him (but not always), appearing at times as black shadowy figures that can walk through walls or disappear into ceilings. When he comes across a case involving the possession of a person or the extreme infestation of a home by multiple demons, he calls a priest to do a formal exorcism.

Canavan is especially concerned with the number of children in Irish schools who are using Ouija boards and dabbling in the occult, including witchcraft. In an interview with the *Irish Mirror* in 2016, he talked about a case he had just worked on in which, "A girl had been playing with a Ouija board and she met a Zozo demon. It was threatening to kill her friends." By the time Canavan arrived at the girl's house, the demon had been busy terrorizing family members by moving their furniture around. Canavan went on to report: "I went in and did a small investigation to see if there was a spirit and I blessed and cleansed the house . . . I was pushed over as I tried to get rid of it."

Luckily, the cleansing seemed to work, as the girl's family was no longer bothered by any supernatural entities. This case, Canavan points out, is a prime example of how evil spirits worm their way into a person's life. "Sometimes these entities appear as children or as if they are friendly spirits. People assume they are communicating with something that is good and this may not be the case. These dark entities can take on many roles; they are masters of deception.

"I always try my best to discourage people from using the Ouija board, but at the end of the day people will make their own choices."

Chapter 8

Zozo: The Ouija Board Demon

"People who run into Zozo have unhappy stories to tell."

– John Zaffis, paranormal investigator and demonologist

Who or What is Zozo?

It is generally agreed upon by paranormal professionals that Zozo is a demonic entity with powerful abilities to cause physical and psychological harm outside of a "spirit session." Though normally associated with the Ouija board, Zozo has also made contact with people during other spirit-invoking activities such as pendulum sessions, séances, automatic writing stints, electronic voice phenomena (EVP) recordings, and even hypnosis.

The earliest recorded mention of Zozo appeared in *Dictionnaire Infernal* by Jacques Collin de Plancy in 1818, wherein it tells of a young girl in France who was possessed by several demons, one of which had the name Zozo. Reports of the evil spirit were sparse and haphazard through the ensuing decades, but as the use of Ouija boards became more popular in the mid-to-later half of the 20th century, Zozo began creeping into the "conversations" more frequently. As paranormal researcher Rosemary Guiley, in her book *The Zozo Phenomenon*, writes:

"It should be no surprise that a manipulative entity like Zozo has been able to rise in presence and prominence over the past several decades. The proliferation of millions of talking boards and eager human communicators provide plenty of opportunities for enterprising predators to make contact with potential victims."

If there is a single common thread that runs through all reported Zozo encounters, it is this: darkness. A run-in with Zozo causes a person to not only feel afraid but, in many instances, morbidly depressed. A suffocating sense of dread often settles on the victim, and thoughts of self-abuse and suicide are not unusual. The darkness may be external as well, with many people reporting moving shadows, black formless figures, or a room that suddenly gets darker. Other signs that Zozo may be present include:

- The planchette makes rapid figure eights or rainbow-shaped side-to-side movements.

- One or more of the following names are actually spelled out: Zozo, Zaza, Oz, Zo, Za, Mama, and Abacus.

- The power goes out or electronic devices go haywire.

- A terrible smell like rotting meat fills the air.

- It won't let you end the session; it will continually move the planchette to NO when you try to say goodbye.

Many people report that once they are contacted by the Zozo spirit, they continue to be contacted by it, even years later and at different locations. Others report that the demon sometimes "jumps" from its original contactee to someone new. The transference can happen right away, or it can occur months down the road.

Plagues of misfortune, illness, nightmares, frightening visions, and other unsettling paranormal events are common occurrences for those victimized by Zozo. Extreme cases of demonic oppression and possession, necessitating the services of an exorcist, have also been reported.

The easiest way of avoiding Zozo, of course, is to simply not use a Ouija board or other spirit summoning method. But in the event you do find yourself in the unenviable position of being greeted by Zozo, here are some things to keep in mind:

- Don't panic. Dark entities feed off of fear and other negative energy.

- Close the session immediately by moving the planchette to the word GOODBYE.

- Get rid of the Ouija board.

- Do not say the name of the demon or talk about it later. It empowers them.

- Seek the help of clergy or a paranormal professional if trouble persists.

The following encounters with Zozo are terrifying examples of "trouble persisting" and hopefully will discourage any inclination to contact, communicate, or otherwise interact with the infamous "Ouija board demon."

Zozo Comes Calling

Darren had always had an interest in the occult, Ouija boards in particular, but he had to reconsider his activities when things got scary-personal in the mid-1980s. Using an old Ouija board that he found under his girlfriend's house in his hometown of Tulsa, Oklahoma, Darren encountered a spirit that called itself Zozo. At first the spirit was congenial but soon started spelling out foul words and issuing disturbing threats. One night it told Darren it wanted to take his girlfriend, Jamie, to paradise. When Darren asked where that was, Zozo spelled out HELL. Darren quickly ended the session after that.

About a week later, Darren tried out the Ouija board again, hoping that his earlier encounter with Zozo was a one-time occurrence. It wasn't. But this time Zozo didn't appear menacing, and Darren even jokingly asked it what he should name his rock band that he was in the process of putting together. The spirit answered, IRON TONGUE. At the time, Darren thought the name was pretty good. That is, until a horrifying event occurred just days later that left Darren with no doubt as to Zozo's malicious nature.

Darren's one-year-old daughter became sick with an internal infection that had doctors baffled as to its origin or prognosis. She was hospitalized, during which time her tongue swelled up so much it nearly asphyxiated her. It became rock hard, distorted her face, and hung grotesquely from her mouth. Darren immediately recalled his last conversation with Zozo and vowed to never touch the Ouija board again. He and Jamie spent day and night at their daughter's side, praying for her recovery. Thankfully, after two weeks the infection cleared up and the family returned home.

For a while all was peaceful in Darren's house after the hospital incident. But it soon became apparent that Zozo, and possibly other undesirable spirits, had never really left. A new reign of terror began when, one night, loud, guttural laughter awoke Darren and Jamie from a deep sleep. Looking around the bedroom, they could see they were alone, but both admitted to feeling terrified at the sinister tone of the laugh. Other strange things started happening soon after: lights went on and off by themselves, doors opened and closed, objects were tossed across the room by invisible means, and spiders — lots and lots of spiders — appeared everywhere. Friends and relatives who stayed over reported hearing frightening voices coming from inside the walls. And on two separate nights, both Darren and Jamie were awakened by the horrifying sensation of being choked around the neck by invisible hands.

Discouraged and scared, Darren was discussing these ongoing events with a close friend one evening on the back porch of his home. *Are we cursed?* he wondered out loud. To this day, he still doesn't know why or from where he got the sudden inspiration to shout out, "I rebuke this curse in the name of Jesus Christ!" He barely finished the sentence when a loud boom shook the house, causing neighbors to come out and see what had happened. Thinking something had fallen onto the roof, Darren grabbed a ladder, climbed up on top of his house, but saw nothing out of the ordinary, either on the roof, in the yard, or anywhere near the premises.

Darren believes that whatever caused the thundering noise also caused Zozo to go away. For the next few years, Darren and his family experienced a peaceful existence in their home, free of any paranormal disturbances from Zozo or other supernatural entities. Unfortunately, time and circumstances wore down Darren's resolve to never again use a Ouija board, and as we'll see in the next story, that decision brought about a visit from an old acquaintance.

Zozo Returns

Darren had broken up with his girlfriend Jamie and was now living in a small town in central Michigan. He had a new female friend, Linda, and was surprised to learn that she didn't believe in spirits, good or bad. Darren decided, against his better judgment, to make her a believer. He downloaded a Ouija board from the Internet, printed it out, and, using a small glass for a planchette, showed Linda how to summon the spirits. Within minutes the glass started moving over the letters ZOZO.

When Darren's face turned deathly pale, Linda asked him what was wrong. He explained that he had encountered Zozo before. He knew he should have ended the session immediately, but he was curious. Was this the same entity that had terrorized him in Oklahoma? He asked the spirit where it came from. CYBERSPACE, it told him. He tried a different question. Where do you live? SKULL, it spelled. That didn't make much sense to Darren, so he asked again. This time the entity spelled out MIRROR. Right then, Linda's seven-year-old niece, who had been watching with a friend, screamed and pointed to the large mirror in the corner. A necklace with a skull pendant had been draped over the top of it—and the skull was now swaying back and forth. Darren and Linda grabbed the kids and raced out the door into the cold, snowy night. Too scared to know what else to do, they stood out there for twenty minutes before venturing back inside.

Darren wasted no time ripping up the paper Ouija board. But the next day, to Darren's dismay, Linda drove 40 miles to purchase a glow-in-the-dark Ouija board. She admitted she was fascinated by what had happened the night before and wanted to try it out again. Darren reluctantly agreed to be present at the session but made clear that he wasn't going to participate. Linda enlisted the help of her two nieces, and in a matter of minutes, they summoned a spirit claiming to be Zozo.

Darren decided to test the spirit, as well as to make sure it was actually there and not a subconscious action of the players. He wrote down the word "blue" on a piece of paper, folded it, and had Linda ask the board what color he had written down. The planchette quickly spelled out BLUE. Darren wrote down another color. The board guessed correctly again. Then he wrote the names of shapes and other random words. The board spelled out the right word every time. That was enough, Darren decided. He convinced Linda to end the session and get rid of the Ouija board.

While he had no desire to ever contact a "spirit" again by the board or other means, he did want to know more about the harassing entity that had followed him from one state to another. He researched the name Zozo online and was amazed to learn that he wasn't the only one who had been contacted by this spirit. In fact, Darren learned that Zozo is often referred to as "the Ouija demon" because of its ubiquitous presence at spirit board gatherings.

Unfortunately, as Darren knew firsthand, Zozo didn't always stay attached to the Ouija board. Countless testimonies related frightening paranormal experiences, strings of bad luck, unexplained illnesses, horrifying nightmares, and, in some cases, even demonic possession that resulted after encountering Zozo. The deeper he dug, and the more terrifying the reports that he uncovered, the more convinced he became that, as a "Zozo survivor," he needed to let others know about "the Ouija demon."

Darren is now a paranormal researcher and co-author of the book *The Zozo Phenomenon*. He devotes a great deal of his time to warning others about this evil spirit through the use of social media, printed materials, film, and video. Because of his personal experience and years of investigation, Darren is passionate about steering people away from any contact with this spirit.

"Heed my warnings, people. If you are playing around with a Ouija board and you jokingly ask it if it has a name and it spells ZOZO, close the session properly, cleanse the house, NEVER, I repeat, NEVER ask it again . . . It is dangerous beyond words. I realize not every session results in negativity, but when you play with Zozo you are playing with fire."

After Darren's second run-in with Zozo, he moved to a new house in a new city. He had the house blessed and cleansed, and he has since tried to live a positive lifestyle that incorporates regular prayer and church attendance. Though Darren hasn't gone near a Ouija board since that night in Michigan, he says he still occasionally feels Zozo's presence, nothing dramatically terrifying, just a slight awareness that the demon is nearby. It makes him wonder at times if he should stop his crusade against Zozo. But then someone will send him their story, often a heartbreaking one, and his resolve to fight comes back: "I know it will go on... Why shouldn't I remain vigilant against this demon?"

Zozo the Liar

Katie and Sarah had only good intentions when they brought out a Ouija board one crisp autumn night in 2010. Katie had recently lost her father in a car accident and wanted to say a proper goodbye to him. Hoping for the best, the girls darkened the room, lit some candles, and started the session. To their delight, it wasn't long before a spirit they believed to be Katie's father began communicating with them. The spirit answered all their questions with an accuracy and insight that Katie believed only her dad could provide.

Then suddenly the spirit seemed to change — to Sarah's mother! Sarah's mom had died five years earlier from cancer, and Sarah was overcome with emotion at the chance to "speak" with her again. After answering questions that left Sarah, like Katie, with no doubt that she was communicating with her parent, the board indicated that the spirit had "switched" to someone new yet again. The girls asked who was there, and in reply the planchette moved over the letters OZOZOZOZOZOZ over and over again. Calling the spirit Oz, they asked it to prove its presence by blowing out a candle. Before they could even finish their sentence, a candle went out.

Curious but not alarmed yet, the girls pressed the spirit as to who it was. It replied: OZOZOZOZOZO IS MOM DAD. Sarah and Katie looked at each other. Then Katie asked, "How did you know the answers?" Again the planchette moved. READ MINDS, it spelled out. Now a bit alarmed, the girls were about to end the session when their fingertips were guided to move the pointer over more letters, letters that spelled out a vulgar word. This time the girls did end the session, a little scared but mostly angry that this Oz spirit had played upon their emotions and stole from their most private and precious memories.

A few weeks later they took the Ouija out again, thinking that enough time had passed for Oz to move on. Unfortunately, they were wrong. The spirit returned immediately and wasted no time on pleasantries or game-playing. "He was nasty, cursing at us, saying dark things," Katie recalled. The girls had

had enough. They ended the session and tossed the board in the trash. But still they couldn't shake their harasser completely. They both experienced a rash of bad luck in the days that followed, prompting them to research their plight on the Internet. There they learned about the pervasive and malevolent "Ouija demon." The girls were pretty certain their Oz spirit was actually the infamous Zozo. The only question that remained was, how long would it be in their lives?

Zozo Attacks

Amateur ghost hunter Jim, his wife Rene, and their friend Becky were excited at the prospect of exploring their newest "haunt," the ruins of a pre-Civil War mansion just outside Vicksburg, Mississippi. They had arrived shortly after midnight in the midst of a fierce storm and were all too happy to dry off inside the house, even if it was dark and foreboding. After setting up some battery-operated lanterns, the trio unpacked their ghost hunting equipment and got to work. After two hours of failed EVP (electronic voice phenomena) sessions, infrared thermometer readings, and EMF (electromagnetic field) measurements, the group decided to use an old-school technique: a Ouija board.

At Jim's request, Rene sat out the session, as she was pregnant and Jim didn't want to take any unnecessary risks. Then he and Becky settled on opposite sides of the board, placed their fingers on the planchette, and began. "Is there anyone here who wishes to communicate?" Jim asked. After about a minute, the planchette moved to the word YES. Jim asked,

"Are you a human spirit?" The planchette immediately slid to NO. Right then the temperature in the room dropped dramatically, and the atmosphere took on a definite sense of oppressiveness and morbidity. Jim couldn't help but feel like someone, or something, was watching him.

He looked at Becky and Rene for reassurance, gave a slight nod, and proceeded to ask another question. "What is your name?" The planchette moved to the number 6. Jim asked again, more firmly this time, "Tell us your name!" The planchette responded immediately by sliding to the Z and then the O, over and over again. Jim began feeling nauseous and dizzy at this point, but whether it came from external or internal factors, he wasn't sure. He had heard the stories about the Ouija board demon, Zozo, and no way did he want any interaction with it, especially with Rene being in the condition she was.

He was about to close down the session when, to his dismay, Rene spoke up in a taunting voice: "Your name is nothing. You hear me? You're nothing. Tell us something interesting if you really exist." The pointer moved under Jim and Becky's fingers. It spelled out I WANT SON. Enraged, Jim jumped up and swept the board off the table, sending it crashing to the floor. "You're not getting our child, you bastard!" The trio quickly gathered up the rest of their belongings and left the mansion. Jim knew he should have closed the session properly by moving the planchette to GOODBYE, but his emotions had gotten the better of him, and all he could think about was getting his wife and unborn son back to the safety of their apartment.

After they dropped Becky off at her house, Jim and Rene collapsed in their own bed and tried to block out the events of that night. They put on a movie as an added distraction and soon found themselves fading in and out of sleep. Rene couldn't get comfortable and tossed around as much as her large belly allowed. She finally sat up, complaining that her back hurt.

"Of course it hurts, hon, you're pregnant," Jim mumbled into his pillow.

"No, it feels like it's burning."

She lifted up her shirt and had Jim take a look. Aghast, he saw three distinct scratch marks, about six inches each in length, running down the middle of his wife's back. Jim knew from his research in paranormal studies that three occurring oddities are often a sign of the demonic. His mind raced back to the mansion, the Ouija board . . . Zozo. He immediately put anointing oil and holy water on the scratches, and then he and Rene recited prayers of deliverance. Inexplicably, the scratches began to fade within minutes of being ministered to.

Jim and Rene experienced no further trouble after that, and they were blessed with a healthy baby boy 10 weeks later. Jim is now very careful when and how he uses a Ouija board in his ghost hunting adventures. As for Rene, she has a much stronger respect for the spirit world and has learned to never, ever taunt anything that decides to pay a visit.

Don't Make Zozo Angry

Ouija board aficionado Hannah assured her friends that nothing bad would happen. She had been using Ouijas for years and never had a negative spirit come through. What Hannah didn't know that November night in 1999 was that a *very* negative entity was listening in the wings, amused by Hannah's claims, and waiting patiently for the opportunity to end her lucky streak.

Hannah had just moved in with her sister and was celebrating by having her close friends Jess and Maura over. After dinner, Hannah brought out her Ouija board and convinced her skeptical companions to gather around and put their fingers on the planchette. Hannah then started the session by asking, "Ouija, Ouija, Ouija, is anyone there?" The group was silent and still for several moments and then suddenly the pointer started moving slowly over the letters Z and O. "Who are you?" Hannah asked, but the planchette, more rapidly now, only continued to move over the letters Z and O. Hannah changed her question: "What do you want?" The planchette stopped its Z O pattern, then slowly spelled out the word HER. "Who is her?" Hannah asked, to which the board replied, JESS.

Hannah looked over at her friend, who had gone a deathly shade of pale. She nodded encouragement to Jess and then asked, "What do you want with her?" The spirit spelled out, I WANT HER. Then the cursor returned to its frantic sliding between the Z and O, all the while ignoring Hannah's questions of why it wanted her friend. Frustrated and angry,

Jess yelled out, "You pussy!" The planchette stopped abruptly, then slowly spelled out DEATH.

"Jess! Shut up!" Hannah commanded, not wanting to provoke the spirit any further. But she found it increasingly difficult to restrain her own anger. She kept asking the spirit questions about what it wanted, but the answers didn't make any sense. One time it spelled out MAMA, which again didn't make any sense to Hannah, but nonetheless gave her chills. Unable to keep her frustration in check, Hannah cursed at the spirit. Immediately the pointer under her fingers began to feel hot. Maura and Jess felt the heat too and quickly drew back their hands.

Instantly the atmosphere in the room changed. The air was heavy with an ominous, threatening presence. Hannah later recalled that she suddenly didn't feel like herself; it was as if something alien had taken over her emotions. She was frightened at first, but then she felt consumed by an intense hatred. That quickly gave way to hysterical laughter, followed by uncontrolled sobbing. Then the hatred returned, and she gave Jess an evil smile, a smile Hannah knew wasn't of her doing but of whatever was inside her.

Jess and Maura were just about to bolt out of the room when Hannah's sister, who had just come home from her late-night shift and heard the crying and shouting, poked her head in the doorway and asked, "Is everything all right up here?" Instantly, Hannah felt like something deflated inside her. She gave her sister a weary smile and nodded yes. It took a while longer, but eventually Hannah felt like herself again.

Thankfully, nothing happened to her friends that night or in the days that followed.

Hannah threw away her Ouija board the next day. She didn't need further proof that negative spirits can and do come through portals opened by the board. It may not happen right away, she now warns, but it will happen. It might be a vulgar spirit that comes through, it might be a mean spirit, it might even be a mischievous spirit. Or, God forbid, it might be Zozo.

Zozo Sends a Message

Marian was always quick to help out her neighbor, Eve. They had lived next door to each other for over twenty years, had watched each other's children grow up, and been there for each other through all manner of joys and tragedies. So when Eve asked Marian to come over one day to help her "with a problem," Marian didn't hesitate. When she arrived, though, not only was she surprised by the nature of the problem, but with the solution that Eve proposed.

Sitting on Eve's dining room table, along with two glasses of iced tea, was a Ouija board. Marian hadn't seen one of those since she was a teenager and had tried one out with several of her girlfriends at a sleepover. She couldn't remember anything interesting happening; just a lot of laughing and acting silly. Eve saw her neighbor's curious expression and explained that she wanted to use the board to find out if her husband was having an affair. "You're kidding, right?" said Marian. But Eve was dead serious. Marian shrugged and followed her lead.

The two women sat across from each other and placed their fingers on the planchette. Eve began by asking, "Are there any spirits here with us?" Nothing happened, so Eve repeated the question several times. Suddenly the planchette jerked. Then it started circling around the board until it landed on YES. Eve sat up straighter. She asked, "What is your name?" The planchette moved to the letters and spelled out ZOZO. "Okay, Zozo, I need to know something. Can you help me?" Eve asked.

This time the planchette lurched toward Marian and stopped. Eve asked again, "Zozo, can you help us?" The planchette moved and spelled out MARIAN. A look of alarm crossed Marian's face. Eve asked, "What about Marian?" WANT HER, the board replied. Then, startling them both, the planchette jerked wildly back and forth across the board, dragging the women's fingers along in long arcs. This time Marian asked in a loud, fearful voice, "What do you want me for?"

The planchette stopped its wild movements and started to spell again. It wrote BETTY WILL DIE MAY 2. Marian turned ashen. Eve, knowing that Betty was Marian's mother-in-law, turned pale too. Then, like some horrid, sadistic jester, Zozo spelled out HAHAHAHAHAHAHA until the women pushed themselves away from the table and rushed from the room.

As Marian was walking back to her house, still shaken by the Ouija board experience, she couldn't help but feel that there was "something" clinging to her. Something heavy and unpleasant. She entered her back door and saw her adult daughter sitting at the kitchen table. Jessie had stopped by to drop off a dish, and the two of them spent the next half hour catching up on family news. Marian purposely didn't tell Jessie about the Ouija board incident, as she didn't feel the need to worry her unnecessarily. Plus, it was a little embarrassing that an older woman like herself had played around with a slumber party game—to catch a cheating husband, no less!

After Jessie left, Marian couldn't help but notice that she felt "normal" again—that dark, oppressive feeling gone. She silently thanked Jessie for lifting her spirits and vowed to put the Ouija board incident behind her. She was sure she would forget all about it soon enough.

But as the next part of the story shows, Zozo had different plans.

Zozo Follows Through

When Jessie got home later that evening, she was more than ready for bed. Ever since she left her mom's, she felt like she was swimming upstream the whole day. Every movement required extra effort, and every decision was accompanied by a mental fog she couldn't shake no matter how much coffee she drank. Hoping she wasn't coming down with something, and glad she didn't have to go to work the next day, she told her husband she was going to bed early and settled in for the night.

Jessie woke the next morning at 6:00 a.m. to the sensation of covers being pulled off from the bottom of her bed. What was her husband doing home? she wondered. A postal worker, Bill should have left for work an hour ago. Then she looked down and was horrified to see that the covers were being pulled off her bed . . . by no one! In shock, she watched as the unfurled covers moved up and forward until they were over her head. She heard a voice speak into her ear that said, "Hold on!" just as she was completely covered by the bedding.

The next thing Jessie remembered was waking up two hours later. The memory of what had happened earlier came flooding back into her mind and, panic-stricken, she leapt out of bed before it happened again. Overcome with emotion, she sat on the floor of her bedroom and cried. And then she started thinking that maybe the whole incident had been a dream. After all, would she have really gone back to sleep if she was being attacked? Feeling a little better, Jessie went into the bathroom and took a shower. When she came out she went over to make the bed. She pulled the duvet down, and that's when she saw that she hadn't been dreaming. The sheets had been ripped to shreds, like Edward Scissorhands on crack had come calling. She immediately ran downstairs and called Bill to say she had been attacked.

Jessie and her husband decided not to call the police, as they had no description of an actual attacker. For the next week, Jessie refused to go upstairs alone, and she made sure she woke for the day at the same time Bill did. During this time, nothing out of the ordinary occurred, and Jessie started to question herself. Maybe she had had some sort of "episode" and ripped the sheets herself. She had felt sick earlier that day, so who knew?

But then Bill asked her one day whose black cat that was that was sitting at the top of their stairs. Jessie told him she had no idea. When they went to find it, it was gone. Later that evening, he saw the cat again, this time in their hallway. He went to grab it, but it turned and escaped . . . right into the wall! Bill, who was not a believer in the paranormal, told himself he was just seeing shadows. He would not stay an unbeliever for long.

That night he was awakened around 2:00 a.m. by the sound of someone opening the bedroom door. Jessie was snoring lightly beside him, so he knew he was dealing with an intruder. He tried to get up, but he couldn't move for some reason. He tried to yell, but he couldn't speak. Being able to only use his eyes, he lay there helplessly watching as a dark shape moved around the bedroom. Then the shadow came to his side and sat down on the bed next to him. Bill could feel the bed springs going down, and knew then that this was no hallucination. Terror-stricken, he tried to scream again and again, to no avail. After what seemed like an eternity, something finally "popped loose" inside Bill and his screams reached the surface. The presence beside him lifted and vanished just as Jessie sprung awake at his outburst.

The couple immediately left their house and stayed the rest of the night with Jessie's mom. In the morning over breakfast, Jessie and Bill described to Marian the strange events that had plagued them the last few weeks. Though she had hoped to never think about it again, Marian's thoughts instantly went to the Ouija board session she had shared with Eve. She clearly remembered how she hadn't felt "right" afterward, and it sounded like the way Jessie felt after leaving Marian's house that day. Had something "jumped" from mother to daughter that afternoon? A malicious spirit? That Zozo entity?

Feeling guilty for bringing this trouble to her family, Marian called a local minister and arranged for both her house and Jessie's to be cleansed and blessed. Mother and daughter received a personal blessing as well. There were no further paranormal disturbances reported after that. Zozo's demonic run of fun was apparently over, but there remained one piece of unfinished business: Marian's mother-in-law, Betty.

Betty didn't die on May 2, as Zozo predicted. Instead, she had a stroke on that day and died two weeks later from complications.

Chapter 9

Friends and Fiends on Fire Island

*"The forces one deals with are of unknown power
and proportions, and should be left utterly alone. I
have never again attempted—nor will I ever—to
contact the spirit world again."*

– Arnold Copper

In the summer of 1967, architectural designer Arnold Copper underwent a dramatic transformation in his beliefs about the occult. He started as a total skeptic, but events that unfolded at a beach house on Fire Island, New York, that summer turned him into a true believer.

The "psychedelic sixties" were in full swing and interest in the occult was at an all-time high when Arnold and three friends rented their beach house that June. One evening they decided to test the occult waters themselves by fashioning their own Ouija board and holding a séance. It wasn't long before they made contact with a spirit named Zena, who told them she had drowned in a shipwreck in 1873. Zena told them many other details of her life, and after that first night, the men were hooked.

They went on to conduct fourteen more séances over a six-week period that summer, often with other friends and neighbors in attendance. In addition to Zena, the group was also visited by Zena's "evil" sister, Beth, and Beth's lover, a male spirit named Higgins. Slowly, over the course of many weeks, it became clear that the three spirits, when alive, had been involved in a web of deceit, treachery, and possibly murder.

If there are results that can be deemed typical of Ouija board sessions, then the Fire Island séances were par excellence. At various times, the board spelled out profanities, threats, and accusations, usually when Beth was in control. Once, during a run of particularly obscene messages, a glass ashtray holding a lighted candle lifted itself off the table and sailed toward a female friend who was present. Luckily, no one was injured. However, someone was slightly hurt when, during a different session, a large chandelier above the table began flashing on and off before it suddenly tore loose from the ceiling and crashed down. On other occasions, the temperature in the room plummeted; fuzzy apparitions manifested on the scene or, in one instance, in a Polaroid photo; and at least one participant appeared to undergo temporary possession.

One decidedly creepy event that Arnold recalled happening to him was the distinct feeling of someone sitting on the foot of his bed one night after a séance. When he looked, he saw no one there, but he did see an indentation in the covers that would be expected when weighed down. Steeling himself against panic, he became quiet and still. *Detach and observe*, he told himself. *Don't let it sense your fear.* After about thirty seconds, the end of the bed rose by itself to its normal position and stayed that way the rest of the night.

Most distressing to Arnold was a near-death experience that happened away from the Ouija board, but which he felt was tied to it nonetheless. He was driving on the FDR Drive in New York on a beautiful sunny day when suddenly his new car seemed to wrench itself out of his control. Neither the steering wheel nor the brakes responded to his earnest demands. As hard as he pulled at the wheel, an unseen force counteracted him with double the strength. He became a helpless, horrified passenger as the car jumped a small meridian and straddled it for twenty feet, ripping apart the underside of the vehicle before it jumped back down, spun around, and crashed headlong into a concrete bulkhead. "You should be dead," was the reaction of the first police officer on the scene. That thought hounded Arnold for weeks after the crash. As did the warning his girlfriend at the time gave him about making contact with spirits: *they can travel with you.*

The last séance Arnold and his crew conducted was on August 12th. Once again they found themselves talking with Zena, who thanked her "friends" for telling the truth about her. The men immediately knew what she was referring to. The day before, their movie actor friend, Bob, who had been present at one of the séances, had talked about Zena on a television talk show. Bob explained the whole Zena-Beth-Higgins soap opera in detail, relating the story as if it were about living people. Zena had apparently been pleased. NOW I CAN REST, she wrote.

The men started to relax, thinking that this was the end of their journey with Zena. But then she delivered one last, cryptic message: I HAVE BROUGHT YOU GIFT FROM MY GRAVE. Suddenly the energy in the room changed and the men knew that Zena was gone. They left the board and went into the living room where they collapsed on the sofas. But something on the coffee table caught their eyes and brought them immediately back upright. As Arnold described it: "There in the center was a little pool of water, and in it lay a starfish, pulsating rhythmically."

In January 1975, the editor of *House and Garden* magazine, Coralee Leon, met Arnold Copper at a party for professionals in the interior design profession. As the party progressed, Arnold and some of the other guests started sharing their various psychic and paranormal experiences. Leon was fascinated by Arnold's story and the effect it had on his views of life, death, and the hereafter. She urged him to write a book about his experiences, and eventually collaborated with him in writing one. *Psychic Summer* became a popular beach read in the late 70s, helped along by the publisher's tagline: "More terrifying than *The Exorcist* or *The Omen* because it is true."

Arnold Copper's experiences with the Ouija board opened his eyes to how thin the veil is between this world and the next— and how dangerously vulnerable we are when we try to part it.

Chapter 10

A Family's Nightmare
The Story Behind *Veronica*

*"Ouija boards signal a type of consent to demons
and it is difficult to be rid of them once they sense
interest from a human being."*

– Msgr. Charles E. Pope, Washington, DC

In early 1991, in a suburb of Madrid, Spain, 18-year-old Estefania Gutierrez Lazaro met with several friends in an empty room at their school for a very non-academic purpose. For the last several months the girls had been dabbling in the occult, and Estefania had acquired a particular interest in the Ouija board. On this particular day, the group gathered for a séance in an attempt to contact the boyfriend of one of the girls, who had recently died in a motorcycle accident. Estefania was leading the ritual using a homemade Ouija board with a glass for a planchette when suddenly a school nun barged in on them and, furious at what they were doing, grabbed the board and broke it. Witnesses recounted that a strange smoke arose from the shattered pieces of glass and slithered into Estefania's nose and mouth.

For the next six months, Estefania's life became a living hell.

She suffered from seizures and hallucinations. She claimed to see "strange people" inside her family's house, shadowy beings that would appear unexpectedly or who would walk past her bedroom at night. At times she would fly into rages, barking incoherently at her brothers and parents. Concerned and frightened over their daughter's erratic behavior, Estefania's parents took her to multiple doctors, but none could find anything physically wrong with her. In August 1991, Estefania was admitted to a hospital in Madrid, where she eventually succumbed to whatever maladies were causing her body and mind to deteriorate. Her cause of death was never publicly released.

Unfortunately for Estefania's family, whatever it was that was chased their daughter to the grave now turned its attention on them. Mysterious whispering, electrical mishaps, and doors opening and closing by themselves haunted the family for months following Estefania's death. One day a gust of wind blew open the front door, shoving aside large pieces of furniture, knocking over shelves, and shattering decor. A framed photograph of Estefania was blown to the floor. When her father picked it up, the photo inside the frame burst into flames. On another day, youngest son Maximillian was preparing his lunch when he heard a whistling sound behind his head. He turned and saw a sausage impaled on the wall with a sharpened stick. No one else was in the kitchen with him.

Family members, as well as visiting friends and neighbors, reported seeing strange, shadowy figures throughout the house, often sliding about the perimeters of the rooms and then disappearing right into the walls. One night, Estefania's two sisters had a particularly scary encounter with one of these "shadow men." It was after midnight when the girls, who shared a bedroom, heard a whistling sound outside their door. They had heard this sound many times before, but this time it was followed by a spine-chilling groan. Sitting up in their beds, the girls were frozen with fear. Their bedroom was partially illuminated by an outside streetlight, letting them view in horror a dark shadow emerging from a corner of the room. "It was the shape of a man, crawling, dragging itself along the floor. It had a black head, no eyes, no mouth, nothing, and it was crawling toward us," recalled one of the girls. The sisters screamed, and at that same moment all their stuffed animals and dolls that had been neatly arranged on a shelf were thrown forcefully through the air, crashing into the opposite wall amidst shouts and bangs. The melee ended when their parents came rushing in.

These frightening events came to a head in November 1992, when Estefania's mother was nearly suffocated in bed. "I felt a pressure on top of me but there was no one around . . . I then felt a pair of hands grab my feet and then grab my hand. I said [to her husband] 'there's someone here.'" The family had finally had enough and called the police in desperation.

Thinking they were answering a call for an intruder, Chief Inspector Jose Pedro Negri and several other officers arrived at the Lazaro residence at 2:40 a.m. As they pulled up, they found the family waiting outside in the cold for them. Mr. Lazaro proceeded to explain that there were "forces" in the house trying to harm them. His wife was nearly strangled in her sleep, pictures were flying off the wall, and plates were being flung through the air. Mr. Lazaro added that this was nothing new. Loud, unexplained noises and banging sounds went on constantly, and mysterious shadowy beings terrorized them night and day. Mr. Lazaro knew there was a good chance the police would consider him delusional, so when they agreed to go inside and check things out, he allowed himself a bit of hope that they would see for themselves that his family wasn't crazy. It was a hope soon realized.

Inspector Negri and three officers followed the Lazaros inside while the other patrolmen waited outside. Stepping over strewn objects and broken dishes, they went into the master bedroom first, the scene of Mrs. Lazaro's assault. Suddenly they heard a tremendous crash from the direction of the balcony, as if a large boulder had been dropped on the floor. Upon investigation, they found nothing to explain the noise, but even stranger, the officers outside claimed they heard no sound at all. As they talked more with the Lazaros about the strange goings-on, one of the officers shouted for his partner to move. Just as he did, the door of a large pine armoire swung open where moments before the officer had been standing.

On heightened alert, the officers continued their walkabout through the residence. As they neared a bathroom, they were told it was only used for washing clothes and storing dishes because odd things occurred in it. When the officers went in to check for themselves, they reported experiencing a sudden and drastic drop in temperature and hearing disembodied voices. In a small bedroom with two twin beds, Mr. Lazaro recounted a time when he witnessed his son being picked up and flung from one bed to the other across the room. And in still another room, the group watched as a "drool-like" brown substance spread across a tablecloth with no visible point of origin. That was enough for two of the officers, who refused to stay in the house any longer.

In a 2012 documentary, Inspector Negri talked further about what he and his officers experienced in the Lazaro house, calling the events "horrendous." At one point, he recalled, they were talking to Mr. and Mrs. Lazaro about Estefania's sudden and inexplicable death—which they insisted was caused by supernatural forces unleashed by their daughter's Ouija board—when they were interrupted by a loud noise from her bedroom. Rushing in, they saw that a large wooden crucifix, which minutes before had been perfectly intact on the wall, was now upside down, and a smaller crucifix that had been attached to it was lying on the floor. A poster that shared the same space had been shredded with what looked like three or four claw marks that left deep scratches in the wall behind it.

Regrettably, the officers could do little else to help the Lazaro family, as they found no tangible evidence of "an intruder." The official police report would later describe the events that took place in evocative detail, and summarized the call to the residence as "a situation of mystery and rarity." The report remains labeled as "unexplained." In addition to the police, the Lazaro family reached out to clergy and exorcists as well. No one could help them rid their house of the paranormal presence that terrorized them, and shortly thereafter they were forced to move out.

In part because of the official police involvement, the Vallecas Case, as it is widely known, has become somewhat of a legend in Spain. It also attracted the attention of Spanish filmmaker Paco Plaza, who in 2017 used it as the basis of his movie *Veronica*. Released on Netflix in February 2018 with subtitles, *Veronica* made a splash in the entertainment industry, with Netflix advertising it as "the scariest movie ever made."

Whether or not the movie is worthy of the hype is debatable, but for Estefania and her family, no cinematic invention could be more terrifying than the real-life events they experienced after an ill-fated decision to play with a Ouija board.

Chapter 11

When the Author of *The Exorcist* Tried Out a Ouija Board

"The bottom line is to steer well clear of such things. Otherwise the diocesan exorcist may be knocking at your door."

– Fr. John Bollan, Scottish exorcist

Before the movie *Ouija* came out in 2014 (and its sequel which is actually a prequel, *Ouija: Origin of Evil*), the movie that most dramatically depicted the horrific consequences of playing with a spirit board was *The Exorcist*.

Based on the 1971 best-selling novel by William Peter Blatty, *The Exorcist* tells the story of a little girl, Regan, who becomes possessed by a demon after playing around with an old Ouija board she finds in the basement. Early in the film, Regan's mother, Chris, asks her daughter how she's been playing it alone. Regan nonchalantly explains that she's been playing it with "Captain Howdy."

"Who's Captain Howdy?" asks Chris

"You know, I make the questions and he does the answers."

Captain Howdy is, of course, the demon masquerading as Regan's spirit-world playmate.

Topping most lists as the scariest movie ever made (and the scariest book ever written), *The Exorcist* not only made Blatty a star, but opened the door to a whole new generation of horror films, a sub-genre that could be called the "Supernatural Thriller," the likes of which today are reflected in modern hits like *The Exorcism of Emily Rose, The Conjuring,* and the *Paranormal Activity* franchise films.

Blatty also achieved something else with *The Exorcist* that in the early 1970s was considered countercultural, if not downright heretical. He made evil a tangible thing. He personified it. It was something that was real, that was intelligent, that was cunning. Yet it could be confronted and overcome. By religion, of all things! This flew in the face of everything the pop psychology of the time preached: that the concept of evil was outdated, irrelevant, and, if anything, was just a "disordered psychosis" appearing in a few unfortunate individuals.

Blatty held a different opinion. His extensive research into demonic possession, which started after he heard news accounts of an exorcism case involving a 14-year-old Maryland boy in 1949, convinced him that the devil exists and that it does, on rare occasions, possess people. If not the devil itself, then some facsimile. "Now whether that is the spirit of something dead, whether it's a demon, or a devil in the sense of a fallen angel or whether in fact it's just some kind of pure energy, I don't know."

Blatty was once asked by journalist Ray Connolly if he ever frightened himself during the writing of *The Exorcist*. Blatty's answer was surprising and insightful.

"Well, I don't want to sound like a nut, but as I was writing the last chapter and the epilogue I did have a series of bizarre experiences. For the first time in my life I got hung up on a Ouija board for 10 days. I'd never done it before but I found I couldn't leave it alone. And I had the most definite feeling that I was communicating with the dead."

Blatty thought he was, in fact, communicating with his father, and to validate his experience he enlisted the help of a young woman who had psychic abilities. She acted as a medium during the Ouija session by placing her fingers on the planchette while in a self-imposed hypnotic trance. Not touching the board at all himself, Blatty then asked questions in Arabic (he and his father were Lebanese). Though the girl did not know a word of Arabic, the planchette under her fingertips spelled out uncannily accurate answers to all of Blatty's questions.

Even still, he harbored some skepticism. He thought it could be possible that he subconsciously worded the questions in English and his assistant picked them up telepathically.

That theory, dubious as it was, might have been easier to accept if it hadn't also been for the poltergeist activity that occurred afterward.

"Doing revision of the book at a friend's house, the telephone rang and suddenly the receiver leapt off the hook. It happened to him first and then to me. So I asked a friend who did the acoustics for the Kennedy Center what the possibilities were electrically and he said it was impossible. Then telephone engineers in two states confirmed that it was impossible. But we both saw it happen. That was the culmination of several incidents, but it was the one that in no way could be explained."

Unlike this one, apparently.

"An electric typewriter wrote a line of gibberish, but what do I know about electricity. Maybe there was a short circuit somewhere."

William Peter Blatty died on January 12, 2017, at the age of 89, after a short battle with blood cancer.

Chapter 12

A Few Final Words

"I suggest if you have a Ouija board, throw it out."

– Char Margolis, psychic medium

The promise of hidden knowledge has teased and tantalized the human race since the beginning of time. Who wouldn't like to know what the future holds for them? Who isn't interested in what the afterlife is like? And who wouldn't like one last word with a departed loved one?

Most people accept that the answers to such esoteric questions are beyond their earthly grasp. But some people don't. Desperate to contact dead relatives, to learn cosmic secrets, or develop their own psychic abilities, they turn to the occult for wisdom and guidance. In particular, they often turn to that marvelous, modern-age divination sensation —the Ouija board.

And wish they hadn't.

Paranormal investigator, mother, wife, and author Mary Ann Winkowski has the unusual gift of being able to see earthbound spirits—"ghosts"—that are trapped on earth and haven't yet "crossed over." It has given her a unique insight into the spirit world and how we should deal with it.

"What I wish people would understand is that they can easily attract ghosts—and all the problems associated with ghosts— by messing around with metaphysical objects such as Ouija boards, pendulums, or Tarot cards...There is absolutely no reason for average people to attempt these methods of contacting spirits. If any spirits urgently need to communicate with you, they will find a way."

Mary Ann also delivers this warning: "While Ouija boards generally attract the attention of earthbound spirits, they can occasionally invite other entities into a home."

Other entities. Non-human entities. Demons. Why take the chance?

We know from numerous personal testimonies, the experiences of legitimate psychics and mediums, and the knowledge of trained exorcists and clergy that the spirits that come through the Ouija board can't be trusted. The initial contact may seem harmless at first, but it is all part of the grooming process, not unlike what a predator on social media will do to gain the trust of his victim. The spirit will masquerade as the player's dead relative, spell out true statements about the player, reveal intriguing information about past or future events—all in a ploy to manipulate and control the player for its sinister purposes.

Controlling the player is the entity's goal, but it can't be done without the player's consent. Demonologist Adam Blai, who is authorized by the Catholic Church to assist with exorcisms in the diocese of Pittsburgh and who trains priests on a national level in the subject, is blunt about this. "You're giving your rights away," he says when you use a Ouija board or other medium that requires touching or use of a body part. "You're giving dominion over to a spirit to operate part of your body when you're engaging in these practices."

In a fascinating presentation he gave in 2016 entitled "Exorcism in the Modern Church and How to Keep the Doors to the Demonic Closed," Adam recounted a creepy story that perfectly illustrates this assertion.

Adam had been at a meeting where, against his advice, a Ouija board session took place. Afterward, the main player came outside to speak with Adam and reflect on the "scary" spirit session. He sat down on a step and placed his glass of iced tea next to him. Suddenly, the glass started making figure eights on the sidewalk by itself. The shocked player said to Adam, "I'm not doing that!" Adam knew he wasn't, nor was he surprised.

A few minutes later, the player excused himself, saying he had to go to the bathroom. Adam got concerned after 15 minutes had passed and the man hadn't returned. He went inside and found him sitting in a room, looking straight at Adam while his hand was writing feverishly on a pad of paper in his lap. Adam asked if he could see the paper and, again, wasn't too surprised by what he saw. Scrawled over and over, line after line, were the words: *You're mine, you're mine, you'll be with me forever, you said you'd be my friend, you're mine, you're mine.* It took about a year before the player sought, and received, help in detaching his "friend." He had by then reached a point of desperation, as the entity was talking inside his head and otherwise negatively affecting his life.

It's bad enough when these things happen to adults. But what is most disturbing about the prevalent use of the Ouija board is that the victims are so often children and teenagers. Given that the boards are marketed toward kids, this certainly isn't surprising. It was more obvious when brick and mortar toy stores dotted the landscape, but even now a search for the board on Amazon reveals its placement in the Toys and Games category, with a recommended age of 8 and up. Before it went out of business, Toys R Us came out with a limited edition pink Ouija board just for little girls. If that didn't fit the bill, a glow-in-the-dark version was available.

The question begs answering: What are parents thinking who buy these things for their kids? Even if—and it's a big if—playing with the board doesn't invoke some supernatural nasty thing into a child's bedroom, it can, at the very least, seriously disturb the child's mind and possibly plant fears and phobias in their subconscious. There is also the danger of it being a "gateway" to deeper involvement with the occult. Researchers have found that a high percentage of people—young and old—who practiced witchcraft and satanism began their occult journey with the simple Ouija board.

It should be as clear as a New Age crystal by now that the Ouija board is dangerous. It is a magnet for attracting any and all passing spirits—human and demonic—and an invitation to those spirits to cross into the human realm. Can this ever be a good thing? Of course not. The late exorcist for the diocese of Davenport, Iowa, Msgr. Marvin Mottet, compared the Ouija board to "keeping a loaded gun in the house." You never know when it's going to go off, or who will be its victim.

The good news is, it's easy to avoid becoming a victim. Reject the Ouija board in every way possible. Ban it from your house, block it from your children, bypass it at parties —banish it from your life.

Remember, the veil is thin and the demonic is just a hair's breadth away waiting to cross.

Don't give it an invitation.

Selected References

Bagans, Zak. *I Am Haunted: Living Life Through the Dead*. Victory Belt Publishing, 2015. Print.

Blai, Adam. "Exorcism in the Modern Church and How to Keep the Doors to the Demonic Closed." *YouTube*, 8 June 2017. Web.

Blai, Adam C. *Possession, Exorcism, and Hauntings*. 2014. Print.

Burnell, Paul. "Exorcisms on the Rise." *Catholic Education Resource Center*. Web.

Connolly, Ray. "William Peter Blatty, Author of The Exorcist." *Ray Connolly*. Web.

Copper, Arnold and Leon, Coralee. *Psychic Summer*. Dell Publishing, 1976. Print.

Dean, Jon. "Couple Call in Ghostbuster and Vicar After Claiming Demonic Poltergeist Molests Them in Their Sleep." *The Mirror*, 2 July 2015. Web.

Evans, Darren and Rosemary Ellen Guiley. *The Zozo Phenomenon*. Visionary Living, Inc., 2016. Print.

Evans, Darren. *The Zozo Ouija Phenomena*. Web.

"The Extreme Dangers of the Ouija Board." *Bible-Knowledge.com.* Web.

Fellezs, Laurie. "I Messed With a Ouija Board." *Medium*, 31 October 2016. Web.

Gruss, Edmond C. *The Ouija Board: A Doorway to the Occult.* P&R Publishing Co., 1994. Print.

Hintz, Charlie. "Girl Possessed by the Devil Through Ouija Phone App." *Cult of Weird*, 7 October 2015. Web.

Horowitz, Mitch. *Occult America: White House Seances, Ouija Circles, Masons, and the Secret Mystic History of Our Nation.* Random House, 2010. Print.

Hunt, Stoker. *Ouija: The Most Dangerous Game.* Harper & Row, 1985. Print.

Lynott, Laura. "Irish Demon Hunter Says the Evil Beings Exist and are Haunting Rented Family Homes." *Irish Mirror*, 21 October 2016. Web.

Martin, Walter, Jill Martin Rische, and Kurt Van Gorden. *The Kingdom of the Occult.* Thomas Nelson, 2008. Print.

O'Regan, Ann Massey. "How to Protect Yourself From Demons: An Interview With Irish Demonologist Gavin Canavan." *Spooky Isles*, 25 March 2018. Web.

Ray, Rachel. "Leading U.S. Exorcists Explain Huge Increase in Demand for the Rite—and Priests to Carry Them Out." *The Telegraph*, 26 September 2016. Web.

Roberts, Paul. "The Demon Warrior is on the Prowl!" *Sacramento Press*, 27 August 2009. Web.

Rodriguez McRobbie, Linda. "The Strange and Mysterious History of the Ouija Board." *Smithsonian.com*, 7 Oct. 2013. Web.

Schwarz, Rob. "Zozo: A Ouija Board Phenomenon." *Stranger Dimensions*, 19 August 2014. Web.

Stephenson, Kristen. "Haunted Hotel is Now Home to the World's Largest Ouija Board." *Guinness World Records*, 23 January 2017. Web.

Whalen, Andrew. "Is 'Veronica,' The New Netflix Horror Movie, a True Story?" *Newsweek*, 2 March 2018. Web.

Winkowski, Mary Ann. *When Ghosts Speak.* Grand Central Publishing, 2009. Print.

About the Author

John Harker is a freelance journalist and ghostwriter who's been writing and publishing since the 1990s. His own scary experience with a Ouija board as a child in part inspired him to write the *Ouija Board Nightmares* books. He lives with his family in eastern Washington, where the ghosts are dry and dusty.

Visit John's website, johnharkerbooks.com, for updates on new book releases and other information.

Also by John Harker

Demonic Dolls: True Tales of Terrible Toys

Evil Unleashed: True Tales of Spells Gone to Hell and Other Occult Disasters

A Small Request

If you have a few minutes, please consider leaving a brief review of this book. Your input is appreciated by the author and by those stopping by to browse. Thank you!

Printed in Great Britain
by Amazon

50428874R00136